ORIGINATE: BUSINESS DEVELOPMENT FOR LAWYERS

ORIGINATE: BUSINESS DEVELOPMENT FOR LAWYERS

A BETTER APPROACH TO BIGLAW SUCCESS

Michelle Cotter Richards

DEDICATION

To my dad, who showed me that if you don't like the look of what's on the path in front of you, you need to either find a new path or hack your way through. I wish you could have been around to read this.

TABLE OF CONTENTS

Preface A Brave New World? · xi

Part 1   **Biglaw Business Development 1.0** · · · · · · · · · · · · · · · · · 1

Chapter 1   What got you here isn't going to get you
                  anywhere else · 3

Chapter 2   But a new approach might · 7

Chapter 3   How to use this book · 11

Chapter 4   Why Biglaw business development is so painful · · · · · · 13

                  You probably believed the hype. · · · · · · · · · · · · · · · 14

                  The hype used to be true. · 18

                  It's not why you went to law school · · · · · · · · · · · · 21

Part II   **Biglaw Business Development 2.0** · · · · · · · · · · · · · · · · 27

Chapter 5   Create personally meaningful business
                  development goals · 29

           Make goals meaningful. · · · · · · · · · · · · · · · · · · · 32

Chapter 6   Identify the Unique Value Proposition You Offer
           to Potential Clients · 34

           Your unique value proposition. · · · · · · · · · · · · · · · 34

           Your firm's unique value proposition. · · · · · · · · · · 42

Chapter 7   Identify your ideal clients· 44

           Figure out *who* your ideal clients are. · · · · · · · · · · · 45

           Figure out *where* your ideal clients are. · · · · · · · · · 47

Chapter 8   Plan · 56

           Time is not a renewable resource. · · · · · · · · · · · · · 56

           "Create" time through the magic of delegation. · · · 57

           "Create" time through the magic of
           boundary-setting. · 59

           How should you use your business
           development time?· 59

           How will you make sure you do anything? · · · · · · · 63

Chapter 9   Sell · 65

           Sell like you will deliver. · 66

Chapter 10 Analyze · 72

           Record · 72

Reflect · 72

Rework · 73

The magic of 90 days. · 75

Conclusion Step Into the Arena (I'll Come With You) · · · 79

Your Turn · 81

Acknowledgements · 83

About the Author · 85

Notes · 87

PREFACE

A BRAVE NEW WORLD?

Let's cut to the chase: You didn't go to law school to develop business. I know. Me either. And yet here we are. If you want to succeed in Biglaw, business development is no longer optional. Gone are the days of finders, minders, and grinders. In modern Biglaw, everyone needs to learn to be a finder.

Don't get me wrong – Biglaw has always valued and rewarded business development. The difference now is that – quite simply – there really is no way to be successful at Biglaw if you don't originate work.

Still with me? Great. Chances are, if you are reading this book, you are among the many talented lawyers at Biglaw who want to learn how to develop business so they can stop worrying about losing their jobs, gain more control of their time and their work, and increase their compensation.

You are probably also wondering why it seems so hard to develop business. Simply put: You don't want to, you don't know how, and you are hoping beyond hope that things will go back to "the way they were" if you just wait "it" out long enough.

That might all be true, but I have a better proposition for you – read these chapters, experiment with this approach, and see if you just can't make a go of this "business development thing." The truth is, you will either do great at it and put yourself on the path to getting everything you want out of your legal career; or, you will find out that business development is most definitely not for you, at which point, you can invest your time and energy into something that is.

Either way, at least you'll know. So read on, and let's see where you end up.

PART 1

BIGLAW BUSINESS DEVELOPMENT 1.0

The jury is in and everyone knows the verdict: There is simply no way to be successful in Biglaw without developing business.

If you think you might be the exception to the rule, I can tell you, you're not. Or at least, not for long. For some reason or another – strong relationships with powerful people, subject matter expertise, an unlimited trove of innovative limericks – you might have a current reprieve, but before long you, too, will start to ask the questions that everyone at Biglaw without enough business asks:

- Are they going to fire me? Reduce my salary?
- What if Bill leaves? Would he take me with him?
- Maybe I should look for a job in-house? But maybe the hours are the same, and how big is the pay cut?
- What about the government?
- Maybe I should consider non-legal options?

No one likes to feel vulnerable, especially not smart, talented individuals who have worked their hearts out their entire careers and are at the top of their game. And while nearly every lawyer I know has experienced those feelings at some point in their career, very few choose to do something about it.

My use of the word *choose* is intentional: As I tell my clients, choice is power, and if you want to put yourself back in the driver's seat of your life, you have to find the choice in a given situation and act on it. At the beginning, it is truly binary. You can choose to continue to do what you have always done, in the hope that things will either improve or go back to the "way they were."

Or you can view the current changes and challenges in the legal industry as an opportunity. An opportunity to create a path forward that:

- Puts you in charge of your time.
- Enables you to do work that builds on your strengths and interests.
- Enables you to earn the compensation you deserve.
- Enables you to provide true service and cutting-edge insights to your clients, who will clamor to work with you.
- Will be *uniquely yours* and one that will bring you satisfaction and pride.

But before I posit a better, more effective way to develop business, let's spend a few minutes to try and understand how we all got here in the first place.

CHAPTER 1

WHAT GOT YOU HERE ISN'T GOING TO GET YOU ANYWHERE ELSE

The biggest reason that lawyers struggle with business development is that they approach it as they do all other aspects of their legal career. Unfortunately, the skills that have brought them success as lawyers don't produce the same result when applied to business development. Throughout this book, I will share fictionalized accounts of different lawyers' experiences with business development to help make these concepts more tangible and therefore, more actionable. Let's start with our first example – Jean – who might seem eerily familiar.

Jean always did well in school – and really, just about anything she set her mind to. A natural extrovert, Jean has always had a big group of friends and lots of interests outside of school and work. Although she thought about a few other careers – something in politics, consulting, academia – she ended up going to law school because she believed it would enable her to do work that was both important and intellectually challenging. Although she didn't know much about Biglaw, she was attracted to the prestige and financial security it promised, and knew she would be able to replicate the success she had created throughout her life there. Although she got offers from several different firms, she picked the one that included the people she liked the best and some of the practice areas she thought seemed most interesting.

Jean started at Biglaw, and all her predictions of a good fit were spot on. Within the first few weeks of her first year, the powers-that-be identified her as a "superstar," and she got to work with the firm's most powerful lawyers on cases for the firm's most desirable clients. She was quickly named to all of the "cool" committees: Recruiting, associate affairs, women's initiative, and other *ad hoc* committees created to tackle special projects valued by firm leadership. The hours were long and the work was hard, but she was thriving. Her career was on the fast track, and she was learning amazing skills from the leaders in her field. She was promoted, learned how to manage and delegate, and was selected for the firm's leadership development program. Part of Jean's satisfaction stemmed from the relationships she formed with her colleagues and clients and she had a robust network. She wrote articles and blog posts, attended and spoke at conferences, and was invited to help with numerous client pitches. When the time came for her to draft her partner memo, she checked every box and made partner the first time her practice group put her up.

Jean was relieved that all of her hard work had finally paid off. She happily filled out the paperwork with the bank the firm recommended to make the requisite capital contribution. She continued to do all of the things she had always done: Doing great work, building authentic relationships, demonstrating extraordinary firm citizenship. Yet subtly, almost imperceptibly, she began to realize that those things no longer had the same salubrious effect on her career.

In fact, Jean was beginning to think that somewhere, someone had literally raised the bar on her. She raised the issue with the three partners who had been her ardent supporters for nearly 10 years, who, in turn, essentially told her that it was "time she figured it out for herself."

Jean was confused. She had always done everything she was supposed to do, but all of a sudden she felt the momentum surrounding her career grinding to a halt. Her billable hours and reviews were good, so she decided to focus on business development. She went to all the firm trainings on the topic, met with her contacts, and made a few presentations, but it was hard to know if any of it made a difference. She brought in a few smaller clients here and there, but the firm seemed to regard her smattering of bookable revenue as more of a burden than a bounty. She continued to invest in her internal and external relationships, but was having trouble getting significant business out of any of them. She almost brought in a client that would have really helped her move forward, but an influential partner in another office wouldn't let the firm represent Jean's client because he felt it would undermine his relationship with his (much larger) client. Always a team player, Jean understood, but felt like she was running out of options – fast.

Politically savvy, Jean started to sense concern about how she fit into the larger practice group's overall strategy. At her billing rate, it was hard to justify staffing her on other cases, yet she did not have enough work of her own to cover her overhead costs. Additionally, as clients were becoming much more price sensitive and sending less and less work to the firm in general, the partners who used to bring her in on larger matters – with whom she still had a great relationship – were becoming increasingly reluctant to share their work with Jean (or anyone, really). When they did bring other lawyers in, those lawyers tended to be more junior and bill out at a much lower rate.

When Jean shared her concerns with her friends – most of whom had left their firms long ago – they told her it seemed like it was just a matter of time before the hammer came down on her, and she should really start to think about other options. This did not sound like a great solution to Jean. Not only because she knew her income, which was close to $450,000 at this point, would be hard to replace (could she afford to take a 50% pay cut?), but because she did not know anything about in-house work and had never really even considered working for a company. She could easily line up interviews through her connections, but if she did, what would she even say? She also hated the idea of leaving because she had to (instead of because she wanted to).

––––––––

So here we find Jean, in the middle of her long journey of doing everything right, and what does she have to show for it? She knows her finances are in pretty good shape. Although she wishes she had paid off her law school loans, and knows that she should really be putting more money aside for retirement, she has a great house and can afford to send her kids to private school. She has an amazing skill set that makes her really valuable to clients. And she has a big network of internal and external contacts. So, what is Jean missing?

Job security. Jean (rightly) fears that any day could be the day the firm tells her it is time to move on.

True financial security. Although $450,000/year is a lot of money, Jean bills about 2300 hours each year, which translates to at least 2800 hours of actual work (still not including all the time she spends commuting, traveling for matters, non-billable contributions such as committee work, candidate interviews and lunches, preparing speeches, presentations, etc.). That leaves her hourly rate at somewhere around $160, before taxes, which, as a partner, she pays in eight different states.

Time freedom. Jean has very little free time to herself and finds that even when she is "off the clock," her mind continually runs through what she has to do, what she should be doing, and whether she is missing any important calls or emails. She spends time with her family and friends, but not as much as she would like, and she almost never has time to exercise. She vacations with her family, and would like to visit Australia while her kids are still at home, but she is afraid to commit to a long trip because she might have to cancel it. She and her husband have outsourced just about everything, which is fine, but Jean would love to spend more time gardening, playing sports, etc., which she enjoyed doing with her family when she was growing up.

Purpose. For all of Jean's success, there is one question that she absolutely, completely dreads. Unfortunately, it's one that comes up a fair amount: "What do you do?" Obviously, Jean has an accurate answer for it: "SEC enforcement work." But every time she says it, something doesn't feel quite right about it.

CHAPTER 2

BUT A NEW APPROACH MIGHT

> "Change before you have to."
> — JACK WELCH

Does Jean's story sound familiar to you? If you're like most lawyers I know, the answer is most definitely a yes.

What more could Jean possibly do to get what she really wants from her career? She has literally done everything she can think of, including things that have worked so well for her in the past. Therefore, it must not be a question of doing *more* things, but rather a question of doing *totally different* things.

So, what are those different things?

First, Jean needs to stop committing "random acts" of business development.[1] Before she schedules another lunch, agrees to do another speech, or writes another blog post, she needs to sit down, take a breath and create a deliberate, action-oriented (versus idea-oriented) plan to develop business. This will require Jean, among other things, to "press pause" on the reactive, contingency thinking she deploys for client matters, and instead, develop the ability to think proactively and creatively so that she can manage the vast amounts of unknowns that are inherent to originating new legal work.

Second, Jean will have to create habits that make business development a part of her daily work life. This will require Jean to create some

---

1 A great phrase inspired by a great book on this topic: Holz, S. (2008). *Bringin' in the Rain: A Woman Lawyer's Guide to Business Development.* Granite Bay, CA: ClientFocus.

way for her to ensure she does what she plans to do. It will also require Jean to manage her time better by learning how to manage, delegate, set appropriate boundaries, and ask for help.

Third, Jean will have to "pick a horse" – she will have to acknowledge that although she is technically trained to adroitly handle any legal issue that comes her way, she is really exceptional at handling only a narrow band of issues for a specific type of client. This will require Jean to take some time to reflect on what her strengths are, what she has enjoyed doing, and what she really wants for her legal career (and her life) going forward.

This approach is not one that comes easily for most lawyers and integrating it will not happen without a genuine commitment. But adapting this approach for your own practice is far from being an impossible feat.

I help lawyers like Jean put all of this together, so that they not only *succeed* at business development, they actually *enjoy* it. They enjoy serving as trusted advisors for clients they like who do work they admire. They enjoy talking about their work and seize on opportunities to hone their skills, broaden their industry knowledge, and develop relationships every chance they get. They enjoy the benefits of their growing book of business by earning more money, spending more time with their families, friends, and on their personal interests, and taking restorative vacations a few times each year. They enjoy becoming the "go-to" person within their practice area for the work they enjoy the most. They enjoy cultivating their robust referral network. They enjoy working with their colleagues in different offices, and develop authentic relationships based on mutual trust and respect. They enjoy the tangible benefits of cross-selling that those relationships create. They enjoy working for a prestigious firm, serving prestigious clients, and operating at the top of their game.

The goal of this book to help you put together your own approach to business development, so that you can succeed at Biglaw on your own terms and build whatever kind of Biglaw career you have in mind.

———

Now, let's check back in with Jean and see what the impact of a different approach to business development might be.

Imagine if Jean made one slight pivot and – instead of focusing on all of the countless things she thought she was *supposed* to do – she focused on what she *wanted* to do. For Jean, who feels confident about her mastery of SEC enforcement issues, and has built her practice on her strengths, her path might not look that different from the outside. But from the inside, Jean would have a powerful filter that would enable her to focus relentlessly on the things she needed to do to advance her career.

That version of Jean might say, "I would love to help with the hiring committee, but I really need that time to focus on developing business, because we all know that's what's most important anyway." That version of Jean would not settle for a secretary who can't manage her schedule. That version of Jean would not cancel her weekly business development time because of an "urgent," previously un-communicated internal deadline. That version of Jean would regard her partners' short-sighted approach to staffing their cases as an opportunity to educate them about the proven financial benefits of effective team management (to say nothing of cross-selling), and encourage them to develop the related essential skills to do so. That version of Jean would respect her own time enough to work less, take vacations, and spend more time doing whatever she wants. And that version of Jean would do all of this without an ounce of fear, because she would be secure in the knowledge that even if her current firm failed to acknowledge or see her true value, she could easily make that case to another law firm.

Or maybe even strike out on her own.

––––––

Far-fetched, right? If you operate under the existing business development model and continue to approach business development in the same manner you always have, it likely is. But if you commit to doing the different things I set forth in this book, it most certainly is not.

Will it be easy to do things differently than almost everyone around you? No. Will your colleagues observe your efforts with awe and admiration? Not at first. Is it a steep learning curve that will be tricky to get the hang of? Definitely. But you know who will love it? Your *clients*. Because the approach described in this book is completely focused not on you, but on *them*: What they want, what they need, and how you will show them you are the best one to deliver it.

Now, if the way things are shaking out for you at Biglaw are "okay," or "fine," or "tolerable," or if you simply don't believe there's anything you can do to change the trajectory of your career, then no need to read any further.

But if you have the slightest notion that there must be "a better way to do Biglaw," and you're tired of waiting for clients to (more or less) fall from the sky, then read on to see if this approach works for you. And when it does, I hope you'll tell me about it, because nothing makes me happier than successful lawyers rocking out at Biglaw.

CHAPTER 3

HOW TO USE THIS BOOK

In the following pages, I break down the business development approach I use with lawyers into six sequential steps. The most essential steps are the first (goal setting) and the last (evaluating your results). You will get the most out of the book by working through it sequentially, but you can also tackle each step on its own, based on your evaluation of your own needs, strengths, and challenges.

So, if you are really anxious to get started, I encourage you to start with Chapter 5, follow with whichever chapter resonates most, and conclude with Chapter 10. I include targeted exercises and fictionalized anecdotes throughout to help make the concepts tangible and give you the chance to integrate the ideas into your own practice.

To help you do just that (and to thank you for reading *Originate*), I have also set up a toolkit to share some of the resources I use with my clients. There you will find:

- A checklist, bottom-lining the key takeaways from *Originate*.
- A series of two-minute videos that will help you start to develop business right away.
- A customizable business development plan incorporating the *Originate* approach.

You can access these resources by visiting www.originatebd.com

If you want to learn more about how to create your own approach to business development, you can reach me at mcr@mcrstratgies.com, (202) 394-5091, or through my website: mcrstrategies.com.

CHAPTER 4

WHY BIGLAW BUSINESS DEVELOPMENT IS SO PAINFUL

I f I had known that you needed to develop business to succeed as a lawyer, I would have gone to medical school. (But not business school, because why would anyone need a degree in business, anyway?)

Full disclosure: As a first generation American, and a first generation professional, I really only had two career options – doctor or lawyer. I chose lawyer (at the age of 10, after careful consideration of a variety of television role models) because I wanted to be the smart, eloquent, champion of individual rights and justice for all that seemed to be the highest and best use of my fictional future self. I wanted to be in charge of my life, free from financial pressure, and able to use my time as I saw fit: Whether trying cases to a jury, shuttling around the world to solve the most pressing economic and political problems, or taking amazing vacations with my loving, witty, and attractive family. I have come to think of this as my TV Lawyer Fantasy.

Not all lawyers share this particular idealized version of the practice of law (other versions include: The Startup Lawyer Fantasy, the Supreme Court Justice Lawyer Fantasy, the Just Like Mom/Dad Lawyer Fantasy, the Lawyer-Turned-CEO Fantasy, the Lawyer-Turned-Baker Fantasy, etc.). I have found that all lawyers *do* have some fantasy about how a career in the law would put them in the driver's seat of their own life and enable them to become highly regarded, well-compensated, and in control of their own time and priorities.

YOU PROBABLY BELIEVED THE HYPE.

If you're reading this book, chances are that, no matter which fantasy you were operating under when you enrolled in law school, the fantasy you're operating under now is the one I call the Biglaw Fantasy. And that one goes something like this: If you go to the best law school that will accept you, and get a job at the best law firm that will hire you, and do the best work you can for partners that choose to work with you, then you will be successful. Note that "successful" is an undefined term in this fantasy.

When I started as a summer associate in 2000, I believed this fantasy. When I left Biglaw in 2007, I believed this fantasy. Then I started coaching lawyers who had been fired from Biglaw, and I realized that the Biglaw fantasy was just as fictional as any of the others. But this one had *no upside*.

I will never forget my first experiences at my Biglaw – then known as Howrey Simon – still one of my favorite professional experiences ever. I was beyond honored and excited to start my legal career at such a great law firm. My plan was to do amazing work, and use my Irish charm to build strong relationships, and make partner (early). I didn't have a clear vision of what my day to day life would be like, but I knew I was at the beginning of a path that was going to lead me to amazing things: Prestige, financial rewards, intellectual challenges, deep impact, and lots of time in front of judges, juries, and clients. Most of all, I was going to do everything I could to take the proverbial bull by the horns and be in charge of my own success. After all, in every other environment I had been, I quickly made my way to the top – and the sooner I got there, the more options I created.

So the plan was to replicate that. And you know, what? I did. My usual approach worked. I quickly became the go-to associate for some of the most powerful partners in the firm. I moved into a place where I could choose the work I wanted to do, and staff cases as I saw fit. I sought out and developed relationships with the partners I most admired. I moved up the ranks, got great bonuses, was asked to serve on all of the cool committees, and many of my cases were turning up on the front pages of national newspapers (which, of course, wasn't great for the clients, but it was excellent for me).

I began to notice, however, that the more successful I became, the less control I had over my time and even what I was doing. After becoming a senior associate, I started to look around at my colleagues who made partner and realized that – although it was the obvious next step and about 80% of me wanted it for that reason alone – it actually didn't look that appealing up close. Most of the partners (new and not so new) did not seem happy. They did not seem in control. They had to get a loan to give money to the law firm after making partner. In fact, the more I learned about Biglaw partnership, the more it looked like a pie-eating contest where the reward was…more pie.

It was around that time I realized that I was following a well-hewn path to a destination that did not seem all that desirable, and that more of the same approach wasn't going to get me the kind of success I wanted. And what's more, when I talked to my colleagues about my concerns, not a single one disagreed with me.

People had a variety of reactions, including "Well, that's just the way it is," "It's not like you can get paid this much to do something fun," "The firm (or the legal system) will never change," "What else are you going to do? It's not like we can go back and get a medical degree," "I'll just wait until _____ (some external event, like when "we have kids," "my spouse makes partner," "I pay off my law school loans," etc.) and then I'll figure it out."

This consensus really bothered me, but there didn't seem to be anything I, or anyone, could do about it – which was strange, given how potent we all appeared to be. I concluded that the problem must be the profession I had chosen, and that if I wanted to succeed on my own terms, I would need to look elsewhere. So I quit. And I regret that. Because it turns out there was a better way forward, but I had let the Biglaw fantasy obscure my view of that path.

BIGLAW REALITY

Initially, I suspected something was amiss with Biglaw because I couldn't make it work for me. But it wasn't until I started coaching lawyers who had been fired from Biglaw that I realized something critical: Biglaw wasn't working for *anyone*. Except, that is, the *lawyers who knew how to develop business*.

In my work (known as outplacement), virtually every large firm hired our company to help terminated lawyers find their next job. The vast majority of these lawyers were partners, and exquisitely credentialed. Other than that, the only common denominator among them was that they were not *consistently* bringing in new work (even though many of them had substantial books of business). What I realized then was that these talented, earnest, and often nationally-recognized lawyers had approached their careers with the same assumption I did: If you do good work, you will have a long and successful Biglaw career. And just like me, they were all wrong.

But if I didn't know the answer, and they didn't know the answer, who did? I decided to see if I could figure out why "success" at Biglaw had become so elusive. I talked with Biglaw attorneys at all levels, Biglaw leadership, law firm consultants, and business and professional development consultants. The more I listened, the more I heard the same things: Starting salaries were too high, overall compensation was too stratified, partners defected (along with their portable business) too frequently, clients were too price sensitive, and were trending toward hiring too many lawyers in-house, there was too much competition from low-cost or non-legal service providers, law firms were too resistant to change, the billable-hour model was counterproductive, and so on. I found all of this information really interesting, but none of it answered my question: What could individual lawyers do to succeed in the midst of (or more likely, in spite of) all of these external challenges?

There was one topic that came up consistently, and it seemed to be one that individual lawyers *could* work on. It was the same topic that came up in all the work I did with my clients. And that one topic was: *Business development.* When I got people talking about business development, a clear consensus emerged: It was no longer optional, and no one really knew how to do it. So, I decided to figure out the best approach to legal business development and then teach it to other lawyers. I reflected on my decade of experience coaching lawyers. I asked in-house counsel what they *really* wanted from their lawyers. I researched the prevailing best business development practices for lawyers and other professional services providers. I acquainted myself with the research regarding the traits and behaviors that seem to make lawyers unique.[2]

What I discovered was that the skills lawyers need to master business development are *not* natural to them, and they neither learn them in law school or in legal practice. That's the bad news. The good news is that anyone can learn these skills, which is especially good news for lawyers, who are the fastest learners around.

These experiences and insights led me to create the approach to business development you'll learn about in the following chapters, but the following account of one lawyer's experience with the approach is a great illustration of how it works.

A BETTER APPROACH TO BigLaw BUSINESS DEVELOPMENT.

Maggie is a partner at the same AmLaw 50 firm she has been with since she was a summer associate. She has always done good work. Although she is deeply introverted, she has developed relationships (over time) with her colleagues. But around the time she became an equity partner, she noticed the work she was getting from other partners was starting to curtail (for a variety of reasons). She was feeling increasingly dependent on the firm, and did not see a sustainable way forward. Maggie realized that she needed to create her own path forward, and sought to do just that.

Maggie decided to start building out a practice niche that was rooted in her existing expertise and contacts, but which was also personally very interesting to her. The niche happened to be based on a very arcane federal regulatory area. No one at the firm cared much about her new approach (and some were annoyed about her being less available to meet

---

2 See generally, Richard, L., Ph.D. (2002). Herding Cats: The Lawyer Personality Revealed. *Report to Legal Management*, 29(11); Daicoff, S. S. (2004). *Lawyer, know thyself: A psychological analysis of* personality strengths and weaknesses. Washington, D.C.: American Psychological Association; Krieger, L. S., & Sheldon, K. M. (2015). What Makes Lawyers Happy? Transcending the Anecdotes with Data from 6200 Lawyers. *The George Washington Law Review*, 83(2); Sheldon, K. M., & Krieger, L. S. (2014). Service job lawyers are happier than money job lawyers, despite their lower income. *The Journal of Positive Psychology*, 9(3), 219-226; Krill, P. R., Johnson, R., & Albert, L. (2016). The Prevalence of Substance Use and Other Mental Health Concerns Among American Attorneys. *Journal of Addiction Medicine*, 10(1), 46-52.

their current client needs), but it was not misaligned with the firm's overall strategy.

Maggie worked away and built up a small client base and a large expertise. Her compensation more or less stayed the same, but as she cultivated this niche, she gained additional control over her time and her work, which in turn led her to feel more confident and self-assured. With a clear vision of her ideal client fixed in her mind, she was able to make tactical decisions about which business development opportunities to pursue and which relationships to nurture. She tracked her efforts so she could evaluate what was working and what wasn't. Building on this momentum, she was able to develop relationships with other lawyers within the firm, and eventually with their clients. As her workload grew, she reached into other firm practice areas to staff her cases. Through that internal networking, she created additional opportunities to teach others about the work she did, and what she could do for their clients. Over time, about 30% of her revenue came from these cross-selling opportunities, which added to her ability to control her own time and work.

Then a regulatory change occurred – and Maggie's redheaded stepchild of a niche became critical for most large companies to tend to. Maggie's phone started ringing off the hook (her clients are pretty old school), and she was able to work with her firm to capitalize on all of the new opportunities. Some lawyers viewed Maggie's enviable position as a windfall, and concluded that she was "lucky" to be in the "right place at the right time." But Maggie knew better. While the regulatory overhaul was providential, Maggie knew the real reason for her success: She developed a strategic business development plan that aligned her interests and strengths with the needs of her ideal clients – and then consistently, strategically, and deliberately executed that plan.

THE HYPE USED TO BE TRUE.

As the world economy and the correlative demand for legal services continue to adjust to increasing volatility and uncertainty, the core propositions on which the Biglaw model is based are also in flux. The traditional Biglaw approach to doing business no longer works. It doesn't work for the individual lawyers, who are vulnerable unless they originate their own work. Neither does it work for the law firms, which aren't sure how to guide their fleets of talented and highly compensated lawyers toward consistent profitability. And it certainly doesn't work for the clients, who constantly struggle to find lawyers who they can partner with to develop innovative solutions to their most pressing business problems.

How did we get here? Let's find out, as we pour one out for Biglaw of yore.

THE BIRTH OF BIGLAW

In his excellent book, *Glass Half Full*, law professor Benjamin Barton presents a very compelling analysis of the origins and challenges of the legal profession, along with some truly innovative and optimistic solutions.[3] It is no secret that the existing Biglaw model of training (and hiring) has been in place for some time. However, it was not until I read Professor Barton's engaging book that I realized the approach to lawyer development and training in place at Biglaw today is remarkably similar to the system hatched from the clever and extraordinarily well-credentialed brain of one Paul Cravath in...*1899.*

Many law firms were growing in size towards the end of the nineteenth century, but Cravath's innovation was to hire young lawyers directly out of law school, and institutionalize the training they would otherwise receive through varied apprenticeships in their early careers. Was Cravath motivated by a desire to spare Harvard Law School's best and brightest from having to slog their way through the 19th-century equivalent of small claims court? Maybe. What is more likely is that Cravath's innovation was driven – like all worthy innovations in a customer service industry – by an opportunity to differentiate his firm by providing extraordinary client service.

You see, Cravath had an enviable client list: Bethlehem Steel, B&O Railroad, and Studebaker Corporation, just to name a few.[4] But as the economy adjusted in the wake of the industrial revolution, the legal needs of these clients was growing at a breakneck pace. What better way to expand

---

3 Barton, Benjamin H. (2015). *Glass Half Full: The Decline and Rebirth of the Legal Profession.* Oxford: Oxford University Press.

4 Swaine, R. T. (1064). *The Cravath Firm and Its Predecessors 1819-1947 (Vol. 1).* New York: Ad Press.

your services to those clients than to create a pipeline of lawyers in your very own image, who will learn exactly how to serve their precise needs? To say nothing of the revenue benefits to the partnership as a result of the leverage created by adding a virtual fleet of non-equity lawyers, of course. And we can credit Cravath with creating another signature piece of Biglaw. Instead of hiring partners externally, Cravath fostered a "tournament" of sorts among junior lawyers. The lawyers that prevailed earned the right to join the partnership ranks.[5] The model proved so successful, that within a few years most other prominent firms had implemented it. And there you have it: The birth (and entrenchment) of Biglaw.

THE EVOLUTION OF BIGLAW

Although Biglaw has had some ups and downs over the last 100 or so years, some permutation of Cravath's model has persisted. But since the early 2000s, the entire market for legal services has genuinely shifted. The institutional client is no more. In its place are multiple clients, all of whom are becoming increasingly price-sensitive. They require that less sophisticated work be outsourced, or they have themselves staffed up so they can perform that work internally. In many cases, they have created processes for acquiring legal services that look a lot like the ones they use to buy office supplies, including RFPs and other such indignities. The overall economy has become increasingly volatile, making clients less likely to initiate matters with high transaction costs (like legal fees) especially ones with uncertain outcomes. An unprecedented generational shift is taking place that directly impacts the way companies hire outside counsel: As Baby Boomer clients retire – at an increasing pace – so, too, does their old approach to buying legal services.

What's more, due to the rise of content marketing and the increasing professional use of social media, the amount of relevant information that is freely available has created a phenomenon of "information parity" between Biglaw attorneys and their clients.[6] This means that clients often know nearly as much about the contours of a legal issue as their

---

5   Barton (2015), 24-25.

6   See generally, Pink, D. H. (2009). *Drive: The surprising truth about what motivates us.* New York: Riverhead Books; Dixon, M., & Adamson, B. (2011). *The challenger sale: Taking control of the customer conversation.* New York: Portfolio/Penguin.

lawyers do. In such an environment, only lawyers that offer truly unique insights are providing something valuable.

The final and perhaps biggest structural obstacle for most lawyers is the fact that practical business development techniques are neither taught by law schools nor law firms. Since 1899 until about 2005, business development skills were not necessary to succeed at Biglaw. If you were a natural salesperson or had great connections (a *finder*), great: You were given full reign to go out and originate work. If selling wasn't your thing, but you were great at managing existing relationships and matters (a *minder*), great: You were partnered with finders so you could take care of their cases while they went out and originated more work. If you were more of a subject matter expert, who relished the technical minutiae of the law (a *grinder*), great: You put your nose to the grindstone, as directed by the minder, and didn't worry about a thing. Whether you were a finder, a minder, or a grinder, the firm was likely to reward you (albeit proportionally) for your efforts. But if you lived up to your end of the bargain, your long-term success at the firm was virtually guaranteed.

But the modern reality is this: All lawyers need to figure out how to become finders. Quickly.

IT'S NOT WHY YOU WENT TO LAW SCHOOL

So now you know that the ability to develop business is a (relatively) new requirement for success at Biglaw. You also know that, as a result, neither law schools nor law firms know how to teach it effectively. And you also know that all of your successes to date have been built on your ability to decide to learn a new skill, followed (very quickly) by your mastery of that skill.

So, if you're so smart, why can't you figure this business development thing out? Well, I'll tell you, but with one caveat: The following should in no way be used as an excuse *not* to develop business. In fact, helping lawyers develop business *in spite* of these challenges, is one of the things I enjoy most in my work.

YOU DON'T (REALLY) WANT TO.

Hello, Biglaw attorney, let me introduce you to....yourself. You might not know this, but a lot of people are trying to sort out whether lawyers are really different from other people, and if so, how.[7] The results are aggregate characterizations, but I share them here because they resonate with the lawyers I have worked with in one way or another.

First, let's turn to the extensive research of trial lawyer-turned Ph.D. I/O psychologist-turned management consultant to the legal stars, Larry Richard (no relation). Dr. Richard collected data about the personality traits of over 1,000 lawyers using a well-accepted assessment known as the Caliper Profile.[8] Dr. Richard's data suggest that a distinct "lawyer personality" does exist, the hallmarks of which are:

- High skepticism (90th percentile) – cynical, judgmental, don't take things at face value;
- High autonomy (89th percentile) – prefer to work alone, resist being managed, struggle with asking for help from others;
- High abstract thinking (82nd percentile) – oriented toward complex, logical analysis, less concerned with practical, straightforward problem solving or decision-making approaches;
- High urgency (71st percentile) – impatient, a constant sense of immediacy;
- Low sociability (12th percentile) – uncomfortable initiating new, close relationships, prefer to spend *professional* time interacting with information instead of people; and
- Low resilience (30th percentile) – defensive, sensitive to feedback/criticism.[9]

Add to these traits the interesting findings of Susan Swaim Daicoff, who based her research on data collected using the Myers-Briggs Type Instrument.[10] Compared to the general population, Daicoff's research indicates that lawyers tend to be more introverted, which in Myers-Briggs

---

7 Sheldon (2015).

8 Richard (2002).

9 Richard (2002).

10 Daicoff (2004).

parlance means that they are more "inner focused" – oriented more towards their own internal thoughts and stimuli rather than those that originate externally (*e.g.*, people, occurrences, sensations, etc.).[11] In the extrovert-dominant world that is U.S. business culture, introverts may appear to be aloof or disconnected from those around them.[12] Daicoff's research also indicates that lawyers favor a decision-making approach that relies on objective logic rather than a more empathetic, subjective approach.[13]

Taken together, this research paints an image of a group of people who possess neither the natural ability nor innate inclination for business development.[14]

As I mentioned, most lawyers did not go to law school to get into sales. Most lawyers went to law school because they wanted to do work that was based on merit (not who they know), that had a noble impact (not just for the money), and that other people viewed as prestigious (above the fray). A common misconception is that Biglaw business development requires lawyers to cast all of this aside and step into the breach by asking people they know to give them money to do work based on their relationships, which totally flies in the face of everything lawyers historically associate with the practice of law. It's no wonder why so many in Biglaw genuinely struggle with business development.

NO ONE (REALLY) SHOWED YOU HOW.

The decline of the apprenticeship model has been discussed widely, but the truth is that most lawyers still learn the intricacies of being a lawyer by working with other lawyers. For most lawyers, who excelled in the structure of school and knew they were doing well by virtue of their grades, awards, and other forms of external recognition, it is

11 Daicoff (2004).

12 Cain, S. (2013). *Quiet: The power of introverts in a world that can't stop talking.* New York: Broadway Books.

13 Cain (2013).

14 These dispositions and traits may also account for the major sources of client complaints about their lawyers: a lack of empathy and related poor communication skills. Cunningham, C. D. (2013). What Do Clients Want from Their Lawyers? *Journal of Dispute Resolution,* 2013(1).

hard to imagine that you are cultivating valuable skill sets and expertise by essentially learning on the job. But that is where the proverbial rubber hits the road. The very nature of learning to be a lawyer means walking your own path, having your own unique trial and error experiences, working on different issues for different clients in different contexts. Therein lies both the blessing and the curse of the apprenticeship model. By its very structure, the apprenticeship model enables lawyers to develop highly individualized and valuable skill sets. But at the same time, it prevents them from being able to see the unique value of those skill sets.

I am actually a huge supporter of the apprenticeship model for transferring hard-earned legal expertise to developing lawyers. My favorite memories from my days as a lawyer all come from the time I spent talking through questions with senior lawyers, getting their feedback, and watching them in action. It is an amazing way to learn as complicated and nuanced a craft as the law. But...

I routinely seek out successful rainmakers to learn what they do *differently* so that I can bring those best practices to my clients. There are some commonalities, i.e. they nurture relationships and really understand the value they bring to clients, but the biggest thing they have in common is that *none of them* will claim to know how to teach other lawyers how to replicate their success. They can teach you – in excruciating detail – how to set up an extremely complicated purchase agreement, take a deposition, or negotiate with a regulator. Ask them to show you how to develop business, however, and they will draw a blank.

It's as though they believe their business development success is completely serendipitous, and although it's not something they can teach you, they sure hope you can figure it out for yourself. They were not themselves *taught*, in most cases. And the reality is, with the changes in the legal market, even if they could teach you the approach they took (i.e., wait for a "relationship" partner to retire), it probably wouldn't work anymore, anyway.

So, while the apprenticeship model has its advantages, teaching lawyers to develop business is not among them.

You Don't (Really) Care About "Business."

If I had a dollar for every time I heard a lawyer remark, upon being confronted with some marginally difficult numerical equation: "I'm not good with numbers, that's why I went to law school," I would have, well, maybe $200 (if only because, generally speaking, lawyers don't freely admit when they aren't good at something). But that aversion to "math" spreads over to a general ambivalence to "business," which is shared by nearly all lawyers.

Most lawyers won't come out and say it, but if you ask them questions about what their non-lawyer friends do or the inner workings of their clients, it becomes apparent very quickly that they are pretty hazy about how the whole "business" thing operates, to the extent they think about it at all. There are many sound and good reasons for this, but it presents a real obstacle in business development. Clients can readily distinguish a lawyer who wants to use their legal skills in service of the client's business goals from a lawyer who just wants to do more legal work.

And it's no mystery who the client would rather hire.

PART II

BIGLAW BUSINESS DEVELOPMENT 2.0

Everyone knows the truism at the heart of every legal career: Law is a relationship business. But there is another, less well-known truism, and one that has become increasingly important over the last 10 years: Law is also a *customer service* business.

The approach I present in this book will guide you to do develop business in a more effective, systematic, and sustainable way by doing these six totally different things:

1. Create (and record) personally *meaningful* business development goals;
2. Identify your specific, unique value proposition based on the intersection of what you are good at and enjoy, and what aligns with the overall strategic direction of your firm;
3. Understand the needs of your ideal clients and figure out where and how to reach them;
4. Develop a detailed, action-oriented plan that spells out what you need to do each week to meet your business development goals;
5. Engage in meaningful, insight-driven conversations with potential clients; and
6. Every 90 days, evaluate your business development results and re-work your goals and plan as necessary.

Read on to find out how to adapt each one of these to your unique situation.

CHAPTER 5

CREATE PERSONALLY MEANINGFUL BUSINESS DEVELOPMENT GOALS

> "Whether you think you can or you
> think you can't, you're right."
> —HENRY FORD

Goal setting is not magical. Until it is.

The number one differentiator between lawyers who develop business and those who don't is this: The successful ones *commit to* developing business. More specifically, they create business development goals and then implement plans to reach those goals. Mountains of research supports what these successful lawyers know: If you don't set a goal, you won't achieve that goal.[15]

Goal setting is uniquely challenging for lawyers, due in part to the fact that one of their key masteries is the ability to shift on a dime. Lawyers are fantastic at adjusting to changing circumstances and still finding a way forward for their clients. Additionally, the nature of legal work (and the billable hour pricing structure) disincentivizes lawyers from devoting time to planning too far in advance, because external circumstances change so rapidly. Better to do just enough to get to the next motion, rather than bill the client to get everything ready for trial when no one really knows whether the case will go that far. This type of "planning to not plan" might work well for client matters, but it is exactly

---

15 See generally: Locke, E. A., & Latham, G. P. (2013). *New developments in goal setting and task performance.* New York: Routledge.

the opposite of what individuals need to do if they want to accomplish something in the future.

Take the example of Steve (a litigator), who knew his longevity at the firm depended on his ability to develop business. When I asked him about his business development goals, he gave me a list of business development *tactics*: Public speaking, blogging, meeting with partners in other offices, and the like. I clarified my question. I wanted him to tell me his specific goal: For example, how much revenue he wanted to originate in the next 12 months. He started laughing. Loudly. "I can't control whether anyone gets sued!" "Of course not," I told him, "but you can control whether or not you'll be one of the first lawyers that comes to their mind when they do."

But to accomplish that, Steve will need goals. And not just *any* goals. If Steve really wants to develop business, he will need to create SMART goals. That is, goals that are specific, measurable, attainable, relevant and time bound. I shared this insight with Steve. Anxious to have an opportunity to speak (he is a litigator, after all), he gamely "played along." Although he had originated only about $300,000 in client revenue over the past three years, he decided to up the *ante* and set a goal to originate $1,000,000 in the next 12 months.

As he had hoped, I was impressed. But just as he was preparing to check the "met with business development coach box," and get back to a juicy motion to compel, I asked him a follow up question: "Why $1,000,000?" Let's see how that played out:

Steve: Because that's a lot of business.
Michelle: How would that much business directly affect you?
Steve: What do you mean?
Michelle: How much more compensation would you receive as a result?
Steve: I would probably get a bonus.
Michelle: How much?
Steve: I'm not sure, but the firm would be happy.
Michelle: What about points, shares, and the like?
Steve: I am not sure, it's kind of a black box.

Michelle: Promotions, more flexible schedule, job security anything like that?

Steve: Sure.

Michelle: Are you trying to build out particular type of expertise? Financial fraud, False Claims Act, anything like that?

Steve: I'm really a generalist.

Michelle: What kind of an impact would $1MM business have on your practice group or your firm?

Steve: Not much.

Michelle: What's the average dollar amount for the matters you work on?

Steve: Totally varies.

Michelle: How many matters and of what kind will you need to bring in to get to $1MM?

Steve: Not sure.

Michelle: How will you staff these new case?

Steve: We have people who could use some work.

Michelle: Do you have the time to train and manage them?

Steve: I can make the time.

Michelle: How much time will you need to make?

Steve: [Silence.]

For someone like Steve, setting a revenue target that reflects a 300% increase in his average originations *would be* an example of magical thinking, and here's why: There is absolutely zero connection between his stated goal, $1MM in new business, and what he is actually trying to accomplish, which is anyone's guess at this point. (Maybe even to Steve himself.)

Although Steve's goal is specific, measurable and time bound, and while it may very well be attainable, it lacks a critical component of the SMART model: It's not yet relevant *to Steve*. Steve has no clear vision of how this goal will impact his life, either positively or negatively. I call goals like his "untethered" because there is nothing tying them to reality and they will be easily discarded in the face of the inevitable obstacles Steve will face on his path to tripling his origination revenue in 12 months.

We all share Steve's challenge: In a perpetually connected world, with endless amounts of choice and distractions, it is really hard to stay focused on and plan for what we want in our future. It's not that we don't want to achieve our future goals, it's just that the demands of the present are so loud and unceasing, it's hard to see past them. There are a number of approaches I use to help my clients set useful goals, but the one that seems to help the most is this: I coach them to set goals that are *meaningful* to them.

MAKE GOALS MEANINGFUL.

The most effective antidote for ineffective (or non-existent) goal setting is to focus on creating goals that are personally meaningful to you. I have found that personally meaningful legal business development goals tend to come in three varieties:

1. ENHANCE YOUR COMPENSATION.

Let's check back in with Steve. Imagine if he opened up that black box surrounding his law firm compensation model (and why shouldn't he?), and determined that he would earn about 10% of the total collected revenue for work he originated. In that case, Steve would know that he could make about $100,000 more this year if he brought in $1MM of new business. Steve realized that this extra income would give a tremendous boost to his retirement and college savings plans. Building on that insight – and the clarifying view Steve had into his future – Steve could look back at his client data and determine that the average revenue he collected for matters he brought in (or would like to bring in) was about $250,000 per matter. As such, Steve realized that he could originate $1MM in business by bringing in about four matters. With this new clarity about exactly what he needed, several great ideas about how to do just that came immediately to mind for him.

The key to goal setting for Steve was to help him understand the tangible, direct compensation benefit that originating work would have for him personally. In some cases, lawyers may find tapping into other sources of motivation equally helpful.

2. CONTROL YOUR TIME.

Although law firms approach compensation in an unending variety of ways, there is a basic formula at the heart of all compensation structures:

Working Attorney Receipts + Origination Credit

–

Compensation + Overhead

= **Net Revenue Per Attorney**

When the result of that equation is positive, the firm is happy. As it approaches zero (or negative)? Not so much.

So, individual lawyers basically have two levers to pull to make the formula work in their favor: They can increase their working attorney receipts (by billing more time *and* maintaining a high realization rate), or they can bring in more work. If your goal is to spend less time working on client matters, and more time doing whatever it is you want to do, then your best bet is to increase the amount of new work you originate.

3. DEVELOP A PRACTICE YOU CARE ABOUT.

Take the case of a talented and dynamic partner named Ben. Ben had risen up the ranks in a very prestigious practice group of a very prestigious law firm. (This following a very prestigious clerkship he got after graduation from a very prestigious law school. And so on.)

Ben's firm had a lockstep compensation model, and Ben did not feel as though he had a financial incentive to develop more business. He was compensated generously for his role as a minder (and sometimes as a grinder) and truly enjoyed his level of responsibility and the collegiality of his colleagues and clients. However, Ben was fast becoming an expert in an area of law that he found increasingly unbearable (let's just say it revolved around a single section of the Internal Revenue Code), but he was a reliable go-to attorney within the firm for those matters. In Ben's case, the goal that motivated his business development efforts was not based on compensation or time as much as his intrinsic desire to develop his expertise in an area that actually interested him.

CHAPTER 6

IDENTIFY THE UNIQUE VALUE PROPOSITION YOU OFFER TO POTENTIAL CLIENTS

> "Where the needs of the world and your
> talents cross; there lies your vocation."
> –ARISTOTLE

The next component of this approach comes down to cultivating these four essential characteristics of successful rainmakers:

1. They know what they are good at;
2. They know what makes them unique (their personal strengths and interests);
3. They know what their firm is good at (competitive advantage); and
4. They create a practice that combines 1), 2), and 3).

In other words, they create a practice that is based on *their* unique value proposition. Read on to find out how you can do the same.

YOUR UNIQUE VALUE PROPOSITION.

If you don't know what you do best, it is virtually impossible to have anything to say to potential clients. Alternatively, if you are the type of lawyer that has many vibrant relationships, but struggles to convert those relationships into clients, a lack of clarity about what unique value you bring to them is often at the root of the problem.

The upside of this part of the approach is that the way to become aware of your expertise involves a tangible, merit-based analysis – which makes it accessible for most lawyers. All you need to do is catalog your accomplishments, past successes, and personal triumphs.

Lawyers – even very successful ones – commonly struggle with seeing themselves as anything other than fungible. I had one client who worked exclusively on Administrative Procedure Act appeals to the D.C. Circuit. He believed that his work, which was highly technical and required a vast amount of accumulated expertise, could "really be done by anyone who took admin law."

The ideal approach is for lawyers to take the good of the apprenticeship model – the individualized, relevant, and finely tuned capabilities they develop; and leave behind the bad – the feeling that simply anyone could do the work they do. The best way to do that is through…guided self-awareness. Or, as I refer to it with my clients who are uncomfortable with such a "hippy-dippy" notion: Self-investigation.

So, where should this investigation start? First, let's gather the relevant facts.

YOUR ACCOMPLISHMENTS.

The most effective way to identify the value you would bring to *future* clients is to examine the value you have already brought to *past* clients. Think back over the last 12 months, and list your top 10 or 15 accomplishments. The devil is in the details, of course, because most lawyers answer that question with some permutation of the following:

"We won summary judgment."

"We got the merger through."

"We finished an internal investigation."

Those are all great outcomes, and I am assuming the clients were happy (although I don't know for sure, but we'll get to that in a minute). But here's why those are not effective ways to think (or talk) about your accomplishments.

THERE'S NO WE IN I.

Yes, that's backwards. And yes, law firms could use a lot more team building work. But the focus of this chapter is to get *you* to identify *your* expertise. By thinking of the work you've done in terms of "we," you will never get a clear grasp of your individual contributions.

At this stage, most lawyers want to throw out the examples they came up with and go back and uncover experiences that revolve solely around their individual work. Don't. First, there is a lot of merit in working with what first comes to your mind. In almost every case, it is the right place to start. Second, almost all lawyers get results for their clients via functional teams. Although most of the work is done individually, it is the sum of the parts that moves the needle for the client. So, instead of "we won summary judgment," find the piece of the work that you were responsible for, like this: "I created and argued a novel theory of market definition that was pivotal to the motion going in our client's favor."

BREAK IT UP.

Once you have a clearer view of your individual contributions, you will need to tie those contributions to specific results that you achieved for the client. If you view your personal accomplishments too broadly, it is virtually impossible to pair your individual contributions with outcomes, which is what past and future clients really care about. "We got the merger through" becomes "I counseled the client about how to identify impacts in non-essential markets which helped the finance team identify the concessions that were key to getting shareholder approval."

IT'S ABOUT CLIENT RESULTS.

Do you know the number one complaint clients have about Biglaw lawyers? I bet you do. It's how much you charge.

Don't get me wrong: Client concerns about the Biglaw pricing structure are legitimate. But one thing that is certain is that lawyers who focus on creating value for their clients have a lot fewer conversations with them about billing rates, discounts, and alternative fee arrangements.

How do you become one of these lawyers? By understanding that the legal services you provide comprise just one tool, among many, that businesses use to solve their problems. Yes, legal services are just a means to an end that companies use to solve their business problems. Keeping that context in mind will help you think about your expertise in a way that enables you to identify the value you bring to your clients *from their perspective.*

Each of the examples I included above was written by someone who views legal work in a vacuum: As if the summary judgment, merger, or internal investigation reflected the end goal of the client. While the client might be pleased by those results, the real question is: How did those results impact the client's business goals? When thinking about your accomplishments, think about how winning summary judgment contributed to the client's ultimate goal, which in almost all cases, will be a solution to a client's business problem.

So, "we finished the internal investigation" becomes "I analyzed the top three areas of concern in an ongoing internal investigation, and expedited the analysis to the client so they could make the right decision about disclosure – which was pivotal as they approached a new round of financing."

So look back at the list of 10-15 accomplishments you created. Now answer the following questions for each one. If, as you review the list, some examples don't work in this format, or thinking about them evokes the feeling of chewing on sand, let those ones go and find other ones. Also keep in mind that a single client/matter/engagement might yield *multiple* key accomplishments.

- What is the name of the accomplishment?
- What was your role in bringing it about?
- What *business* problem did you solve?
- What was the source of that problem (external events, competitors, etc.)?
- What specific steps did you take to solve that problem?
- What did you do differently (than other lawyers) to solve that problem?
- How did that approach result in a positive business outcome (from the client's perspective)?

In the interest of full disclosure – all lawyers struggle mightily with this step. Each lawyer is different, but some of the things that come up for lawyers include:

- "I can't link the work I did to the overall result."
- "I didn't add anything novel."
- "I wouldn't have known how to do it if [other lawyer] had not given me an existing version of one he did."
- "I don't think I should take credit for that."
- "I don't know how the work I do impacts the client's business goals."
- "The client wouldn't agree with my view of the result."

A lot of these concerns relate back to my previous discussion of the apprenticeship model and other aspects of the realities of the legal industry. Only one of them (the perceived variance between the views of the lawyer and the client) is something to tackle head-on. But the bottom line is that for most lawyers, the ability to take ownership of and talk about your accomplishments is simply a neural muscle that needs to be developed.

If it is important for you to develop business, this skill is essential. It will be hard to do at first, but as you create your list, you will eventually re-wire your brain to naturally orient itself to thinking about your work in these terms. It is sort of like running: If you have never run before, one mile seems like a marathon. But after a few short weeks, one mile becomes your warm-up.

Now that you have a working list of your most recent accomplishments and a better sense of your strengths, it's time to figure out which of them brings you joy. Yes, joy!

WHAT DO YOU ENJOY?

"Each to their highest and best use."

This is a quote I got from my mother, and it reflects both her profound wisdom (it is the key to contentment and success) and provocative wit (she seems to bring it out when I am doing something counterproductive, like re-organizing the summer clothes in January). A client of mine once told me it is a distillation of a view from Marx's "Communist Manifesto," which I immediately disregarded as an unsuccessful attempt to get me to let them off the hook from identifying *their* highest and best use(s).

Whatever its origin, it is a powerful concept that resonates even with people, including lawyers, who are unaware of the mountains of psychological and organizational research[16] that support it. You will always be more successful if you do something that you enjoy. And chances are that if you do enjoy doing something, it is because you are either using your strengths to accomplish it or, as I discussed previously, you view the goal as intrinsically, or at least closely tied to something that is personally meaningful to you. In the former case, the means justify the end; in the latter it is the reverse.

In fact, I don't find lawyers resist this idea at all, but once introduced to it, they quickly panic because "I have no idea about what I enjoy, or what my strengths are or what I find meaningful. I never even had hobbies." Now, I don't mean to make light of a lifelong lack of hobbies. A void in your life where you think hobbies should be could certainly be attributable to a lack of self-awareness, life meaning, or even a profound pathology. But, it might also be simply a result of having a limited amount of free time.

In any case, what is more interesting to me is the panic they experience about not having an answer to the question. Good news: When I have plumbed these depths with lawyers, what I have found is not an absence of purpose or meaning in their lives, but rather two distinct things that obscure lawyers' view into who they are and what they care most about.

The first is a lack of self-awareness about what they really care about, or as Daniel Pink might put it, they are disconnected from what is uniquely, intrinsically motivating to them.[17] The second challenge is the chasm between what feels *uniquely* purposeful and meaningful to them,

---

16 See generally, Pink (2009); Seligman, M. E. (2011). *Flourish: A visionary new understanding of happiness and well-being.* New York: Free Press

17 Pink (2009).

and their ability to bring that into their professional lives. So, I help them fix that. And here's how.

I have found that highly skeptical lawyers don't spend a lot of time acquainting themselves with, well, themselves, so I often use a combination of guided self-assessments and various tools to jump-start this process. These resources, some of which are freely available, help lawyers understand their intrinsic motivators and strengths, and provide specific recommendations about how they can deploy them to set and achieve their goals.

On that note, there is one free tool that I encourage all lawyers to use because it is backed by rigorous research, doesn't take long to complete, and is very easy to integrate for even the busiest of lawyers. It is the VIA Character Strengths Survey, (available at https://www.viacharacter. org/survey/account/register, which is the end result of over 15 years of research that originated at the University of Pennsylvania. After you take the survey, you will receive a report that ranks your 24 strengths in order from most used to least used. To see how consciously deploying your strengths will help you with business development (among many other things), pick just one of your top five character strengths and commit to using it in a new way each day for seven days.[18] Research shows that at the end of the week, not only will you be more self-aware about your unique strengths, you will be happier and less depressed.[19]

But there are simple ways to get to the heart of your highest and best use without these resources. Again, it starts with taking an investigative approach to the endeavor.

One approach starts with a pivot off of the work you have already done compiling your accomplishments. Look over that list again. Of the accomplishments you have included, quickly pick the ones that resonate most with you, or the ones that make you feel pleasant or even joyful when you recall them. Reflect about why you picked those from the list, and write down some notes about what it was about those experiences that made you feel positive about them and why. Include anything that stands out for you:

---

18 For other excellent ways to develop your strengths: Polly, S., Britton, K., & Maymin, S. (2015). *Character strengths matter: How to live a full life.* Positive Psychology News.
19 Polly (2015).

- The people you worked with – were they collaborative, hard workers, substantive experts, personable, etc.?
- The client's industry, products, culture, missions, business model, etc.
- The nature of your role – were you involved primarily with strategy/analysis, project management, client relations, managing legal teams and vendors, budgeting, discovery, etc.?
- The duration of your work – did it comprise one long project, multiple discreet projects or a multi-year engagement; did you service all of the needs for one client or individual needs for multiple clients, etc.?
- Did you learn something new or use a skill set that is well-honed for you?

Whatever the reasons, write down as many of them as you can. Then take a second and review what you recorded. Do you see any commonalities? For example, if you highlighted the fact that you learned new things in each of the accomplishments, it is likely that you are someone who values accumulating new or novel knowledge. If your notes mention relationships, you might be someone who can work on anything, as long as it is with the right people. These insights will not only help you understand what kind of work you enjoy and why, but will help you figure out your optimal business development approach (more on that later).

The second approach is more derivative, but can really help you further develop the insights you gained from reviewing your accomplishments. In this approach, I ask clients to put work aside and (despite my earlier rant about hobbies) recall some other experiences in their lives from which they have derived satisfaction. You have free range here. Clients have used everything from serving on the student council, to starting a field hockey team for kids, to taking extraordinary pictures on an African safari. It does not matter what the accomplishment is, or how long ago you experienced it. Create a list of as many satisfying personal accomplishments as you can. Once you have written them all down, analyze them by answering the same questions you answered in the professional accomplishments exercise above.

YOUR FIRM'S UNIQUE VALUE PROPOSITION.

Now that you have a firmer grasp of your own unique value proposition, the next piece in the business development puzzle is:

What does your firm do well and what makes it unique? In the language of marketing professionals everywhere: What is your firm's competitive advantage? And more to the point: How can you use it to *your* advantage?

One of the main things that surprises me is how few lawyers are either aware of, or effectively utilize the amazing business development platforms Biglaw has to offer. I'll talk more about relying on your firm's business development and marketing infrastructure later in the book, but what I want to focus on here is this: As long as you work for Biglaw, you are developing business *as a part of the firm.* For better or worse, you move around in the world with all the trappings (and maybe the baggage) associated with your Biglaw. So, to have an effective business development strategy, you need to figure out how *your firm's* unique value proposition affects *yours*, with the goal of creating alignment between the two.

This part of the business development approach I use with clients – like all the parts – is completely designed to help you, the individual lawyer, develop business. Some lawyers, however, view this part of it with some caution, and even wonder if I am just a deep cover operative for Biglaw's agenda. Quite the contrary: My mission is to empower *individual* attorneys to take charge of their careers by originating business. But guess what? Biglaw happens to also want you to develop business, and has invested in considerable infrastructure and systems to help you do exactly that. The strength of this infrastructure varies by firm, but lawyers who don't plug into it, by aligning their approach with that of their firm, are definitely working against themselves.

To create this type of integrated business development approach, you need to start with the firm's (and, if relevant, the practice group's) stated goals and strategies. The use of the word "stated" there is intentional. In many cases, these strategies aren't all that strategic, don't reflect the true intent of firm leadership, and many are insufficiently specific as to be actionable. That all being said, these plans will provide insight into the overall direction of the firm and enable you to start to think about how to leverage the firm's infrastructure to enhance your unique value proposition. Additionally, these plans often align with the firm's overall advertising and branding strategy, which should be a key part of the foundation of your business development efforts.

CHAPTER 7

IDENTIFY YOUR IDEAL CLIENTS

> "You can do anything, but not everything."
> — DAVID ALLEN

By now, you know why you want to develop business and how much business you want to develop. You know what you're selling. It's time to figure out *who* needs that, and *where* you can find them. In classic marketing parlance, that is an *awareness* challenge: What can you do so that potential clients are aware of your capabilities?

The solution most lawyers implement is the kitchen-sink approach to business development: Do whatever you think will work, whenever you have a moment, until by the sheer grace of Zeus, you end up in the "right place at the right time" and someone actually hires you. That approach might work from time to time, but it won't be enjoyable, and it certainly is not sustainable.

The approach I use with my clients is exactly the *opposite* of the kitchen sink approach: I help them identify the narrow band of potential clients who most need their services. If you develop a clear vision of who you want to reach, figuring out where you can reach them and what to say to them when you do becomes a much easier process. This is a key step, which will enable you to streamline your business development efforts and make the most of your very limited time.

FIGURE OUT *WHO* YOUR IDEAL CLIENTS ARE.

First, an obvious, but often overlooked point. Bringing in Google or Marriott or Ford or any analogous Fortune 50 company should not be the organizing principle of your business development strategy. When I encourage lawyers to dream big, this type of "ideal client" is often what they come up with. Take for example, Jack, a talented, D.C.-based senior associate. Jack was getting his ducks in a row for partnership, and he knew bringing in work was essential. As we worked on the composite of his ideal client (medium-sized businesses with high-tech visa problems), a lightbulb appeared to go off for him.

Jack: "I just remembered that my law school classmate, Jen, is an Assistant General Counsel at Nike!!"

Me: "And?"

Jack: "I am going to see her at my 10-year law school reunion this summer, and I want to develop a strategy for that."

Me: "What problems could you solve for her?"

Jack: "I am sure Nike has business immigration issues."

Me: "Is that the work she does for Nike?"

Jack: "I am not sure."

Me: "When did you last talk with her?"

Jack: "Bar prep."

———

I call this "big fish business development," and it is almost always a waste of time.

"But shouldn't I think big? Aim high and all that?" You ask.

Definitely! But if you have never brought in a client, getting a medium-sized business with high-tech visa issues in the door is thinking big. Additionally, Jack's goal is likely unattainable from where he is now. While I am sure Jen would enjoy catching up with him, he will need to do a lot more nurturing of that relationship before Jack can put her into the "potential clients" category. A goal that is not attainable *prima facie* violates the SMART goals strategy I mentioned earlier, and pursuing such a goal will probably stall Jack's momentum and send him back to the locker room before he's even gotten off the business development block. Metaphorically, at least.

So how do you identify your ideal client? The first step is to go back and review the work you did in the last chapter. Review the accomplishments that *brought you the most satisfaction* and identify the commonalities among the clients involved.

- Were they large or small companies?
- Parents or subsidiaries?
- Publicly traded or private?
- US- or foreign-based?
- What industries do they operate in?
- What is their culture like?
- What is their corporate mission?
- How do they make money? Is their sales model consumer facing, business-to-business or something else?
- Do they make products or services?
- Who regulates them?
- What are the major legal issues they face?
- What economic, geopolitical, and business challenges do they face now and in the future? What are the sources/causes of those challenges?

Once you have the answers to these questions, you have a much better view of what your ideal client looks like.

In Jack's case, when he reviewed his favorite accomplishments, he could see that the ones he enjoyed most were related to helping companies secure the appropriate visas for critical high tech employees. Looking more closely at each of the clients, he realized that he most enjoyed working with medium sized companies, because he liked having easy access to the major decision makers. He enjoyed working for clients in the D.C. area, because it was easy for him to connect with them on an ongoing basis. He realized that he liked companies that were in a particular clean-tech sector, because he was interested in the technology, and the resulting positive environmental impact was meaningful to him.

The last step to creating your ideal client is to check in with your firm to make sure your ideal client will also be regarded as such by the firm. In most cases, the answer will be *yes*, because you are basing the analysis off of prior work you have already done for existing firm clients. In some cases, the answer will be *no*, in which case, you have two choices: Create an alternative ideal client composite, or find a different firm who shares your vision.

FIGURE OUT *WHERE* YOUR IDEAL CLIENTS ARE.

Once you have a sense about *who* your ideal client is, the next challenge is to figure out *where* to find them, so you can create a strategy to reach them and connect with them.

So, where are these elusive ideal clients who have the kinds of problems that only you can solve? Well, they're everywhere. I am sure you have heard all the stories of the unlikely places people find clients: The young partner who snagged a huge chunk of a major government contractor's bid protest work through her relationship with her nanny, whose daughter happened to be an assistant general counsel for the company. The associate who got all the corporate work for a successful startup – after serving on the same co-op board with one of the founders. Or – everyone's favorite business development unicorn – the counsel who brought in a major litigation client from a *blog post*.

Although ideal clients (or the people who can connect you with them) are literally everywhere, *you* certainly can't be. So, how do you decide where to focus your efforts? First, you need to become acquainted with your firm's business development infrastructure.

WHAT CAN YOUR FIRM DO FOR YOU?

All law firms are organized differently, but the people you need to connect with to find your ideal clients likely reside in marketing, business development, professional development, or practice group management.

Yes, by your law firm's infrastructure, I mean real, live people. But take heart, they have access to other (non-people) resources, too.

When I raise this idea with lawyers, they often wonder what use "Bill," the firm's Director of Business Development, could be to their business development efforts. I am always tempted to ask them if it remains a question now that they've heard they what they said, because, of course, the answer is in the question itself.

If you are a lawyer who knows a lot about the law and enjoys serving your clients, but is not so clear about how to sell legal services, who better to talk to than someone whose *entire job function* is to help lawyers sell legal services?

Yes, it will be a challenge to help Bill understand the finer points of your legal experience (whether he really needs to remains an open question).

Yes, it will be a challenge to get Bill's attention when his plate might already be full supporting established rainmakers.

But if you approach Bill as the subject matter expert he is, with the composite(s) of your ideal client in hand, I guarantee you will be blown away at how Bill can help you.

Here are just a few of the things that Bill and his colleagues have down to a science:

- The most effective unique value position of your law firm/practice group.
- Competitive intelligence (insights about services, customers, and competitors to inform overall business development and marketing strategy).
- Deep knowledge of the existing client base and their past, present, and potential business and legal challenges.
- Up to date knowledge of who is pursuing which clients through which contacts for what kind of work.
- The internal firm network, including lawyers and staff at the firm's other offices (as well as their contacts, who might be great potential clients for you).
- Lawyers within the firm who have clients who might also need someone with your expertise (also known as cross-selling).

- The external firm network, i.e. alumni of the firm, firm vendors, past clients of the firm.
- The informal business development support at the firm, including their frontline observations of what the firm's real priorities are, who is working on them, and where there are any gaps that need filling (a source of potential clients for you).
- Data and resources to support alternative pricing structures.
- Developing and preparing proposals and pitches that are compelling to clients and that distinguish you from your competitors.
- Mastery of the existing resources of the firm to support your individual business development efforts – education, training, software, etc.
- Ideas about opportunities for you to build awareness of your capabilities, *e.g.,* placement within publications and blogs, arranging for you to speak at conferences and relevant industry events, opportunities for you to build strategic partnerships, etc.

So, how can you make the most of whatever business development infrastructure your firm has in place?

1. ASK FOR HELP.

The first step is the hardest for most lawyers, who are autonomous and hard-wired to try to figure things out for themselves. Even if you relish all things business development, and can't get enough of legal marketing theory, reinventing the legal business development wheel is not the best use of your time, skills, or relationships. View your commitment to rely on the firm's business development infrastructure like hiring a painter: You could totally do it yourself, but is it really the best use of your time? And will you really do a better job than the painter anyway? The answer to both these questions is, obviously, no.

2. COME PREPARED.

So now that you realize the untapped value of this amazing resource, one note of caution: Your firm's business development infrastructure has limited capacity. As much as these people want to help you succeed, their time is scarce too, so they tend to devote it to lawyers who are committed to succeeding at business development. Demonstrate your commitment by being prepared to discuss your unique value proposition, and any ideas you have about how your strategies align with those of your firm.

3. YOU WILL NEED TO DO THE WORK.

In almost all cases, you will come away from these meetings with – in place of a gold star or an A for effort – a considerable list of things to do, avenues to explore, and people to contact. This is a good thing. But you will also need to make the time to implement these suggestions, or risk losing your credibility as someone who is committed to originating business (and along with it, the precious resource that is their advice and support).

4. VIEW THEM AS AN ONGOING RESOURCE.

Some lawyers plug into this infrastructure, but after one or two meetings, get caught up in the unending demands of legal practice and simply disappear. If you want to get the full benefit of relying on this infrastructure, I would encourage you to check in with them as often as possible. It will not only create the structure and accountability that is crucial for business development success, it will also deepen your relationship with these individuals, which will enable them to be of even more use to you going forward.

5. KEEP IN MIND THAT THEY ARE CONNECTED TO MOST POWERFUL PEOPLE AT THE FIRM.

This is both a blessing and a curse. If they like what you're doing and are motivated to help you, word of your innovation and *chutzpah* will quickly spread to their own internal network (which usually includes practice group leaders, members of the management/executive committee, and in most cases the chief rainmakers, who have all the power anyway). If they find that your efforts are inconsistent or peter out, they will be less likely to speak highly of you to their contacts. Now, as you start originating your own clients and building out your own practice, you will be more immune to the vagaries of the most powerful people at the firm. Regardless, it never hurts for such people to maintain a positive impression of you.

———

Let me underscore the importance of plugging into your firm's business development infrastructure by relating Mark's story. Mark spent a great deal of time researching and staying current on the business and legal needs of a small health care services company he wanted to target. He combed his network and, over time, was able to cultivate a relationship with the deputy general counsel at the company, Kate. He was in the proverbial "right place at the right time" when that company decided to do an acquisition, and Kate happily invited Mark to pitch for the work. The pitch went really well, and Mark was virtually certain that Kate would hire him. However, it turns out that the company decided not to hire Mark, although Kate assured him there would be opportunities in the future. When Mark asked why, Kate told him that she was concerned about the overall organization of Mark's practice group because soon after she met with Mark, Mark's colleague John called Kate to pitch for the same work. Had Mark plugged into the firm's business development support, he and John would have been better able to coordinate their efforts, and Mark likely would have won the work.

THE THREE BEST PLACES TO LOOK FOR CLIENTS.
Now that you know how to get better information about your ideal clients, the second step is to decide how to use that information to find out where these clients actually reside – which will be in one of three places:

YOUR EXISTING CLIENTS.
Most lawyers overlook the fact that the most effective way to originate more work is by deepening your relationships with existing clients. In fact, lawyers

are about three times as likely to bring in work from existing clients as they are from new prospects. It is no mystery why: Biglaw legal services are expensive, and switching firms is risky and time consuming. Clients feel more comfortable retaining lawyers who have already demonstrated that they can successfully, efficiently, and seamlessly solve their problems.

So, wonderful. You are in the enviable position of actually having clients, and now you know that they are, statistically speaking, your best source for more work. Now what?

First, I am going to ask you to do something counterintuitive: You need to evaluate whether and/or how your current clients align with your ideal client profile. Most of your clients will align pretty closely. But for clients that don't, I encourage you to think about whether you enjoy working with them, and whether you are serving them in the way they deserve. If the answer to both questions is yes, go back and add the characteristics of these clients to your ideal client composite (or create another one). If either question elicits a "no," consider whether they might be a better fit for another lawyer you know (more on that below).

YOUR FIRM'S EXISTING CLIENTS.

Here's where things get a little tricky. Originating work from clients of other lawyers within the firm is a thorny topic, and I understand why. In many law firms, lawyers simply do not trust each other or the larger organization. Often, they are genuinely afraid that if they give other lawyers access to their clients, those other lawyers might "steal" their clients and possibly even take them to another firm. A related challenge is that law firm compensation systems often don't incentivize lawyers to find new ways to serve existing clients, because the economic reward for originating new work often goes to the "relationship partner." Most law firms are trying to address these challenges, because they know that creating cultures that foster consistent and authentic collaboration and, yes, cross-selling, is one of the only clear interventions that leads to sustained profitability in an otherwise stagnant market.[20]

---

20 For a comprehensive overview of this principle and its support, two valuable sources are: Gardner, H.K. (2016). *Smart collaboration: how professionals and their firms succeed by breaking down silos.* Boston, MA: Harvard Business Review Press; Normand-Hochman, R. (2013). *Managing talent for success: Talent development in law firms.* UK: Globe.

Putting the "sell" back in "cross-selling."

Originating work from your firm's existing clients is the second most fruitful avenue for you to pursue – but how do you navigate around these obstacles, and locate your ideal clients within the firm's existing client base? In two primary ways. First, you have to develop relationships with the lawyers within your firm who *already have* clients that meet your ideal client composite. Your goal should be to build a genuine connection based on mutual trust and respect, which will help alleviate the other lawyer's concern that you are going to take the client from her.

Second, you have to educate the other lawyer about problems you can solve for their clients *that differ from the problems the other lawyer already handles.* I think of this part as putting the "sell" back in "cross-selling," because it turns the traditional approach to cross-selling on its head. Instead of assuming that your colleagues a) know what you can do for their clients, and b) trust you enough to call you when something comes up – it is essential that you to take strategic action to find and nurture your own cross-selling opportunities.

Let me illustrate the above strategy with an example. Stephanie was a mid-level corporate associate who had never originated any work. Her expertise was structuring joint venture agreements to help private companies effectively manage liability and tax consequences – and she had a personal interest in commercial real estate. Her ideal clients were companies that needed innovative ways to manage liability and tax consequences in commercial real estate transactions. She worked with her firm business development contact, Mia, to identify possible firm clients that aligned with her overall business development strategy and discovered that a partner, Dave, in another office of the firm (whom she had never met) had a few REIT clients that he did public offering work for. Mia had told her that Dave was really busy and tricky to connect with, but that he had a colleague in Stephanie's office who could make the introduction.

Stephanie got in touch with that colleague, who connected her with Dave. They had a few phone conversations, during which Stephanie educated Dave about the business problems his REIT clients had that she could help with. Dave was interested, and invited Stephanie to his office for an in-person meeting. Stephanie knew to treat this as the great opportunity it was, and worked with Mia to create an amazing pitch *for Dave.* The meeting went really well, and Dave brought up some of Stephanie's insights in his interactions with his REIT clients. Stephanie systematically nurtured her relationship with Dave, and in a few months, he found an opportunity for them to jointly meet with one of the REITs who needed help with....*managing liability and tax consequences in a complicated commercial real estate transaction!* The REIT had been using another firm for that work, but really valued Dave, thought highly of his firm, and was impressed by Stephanie's insights. Needless to say, the REIT hired the firm (well, actually, they hired Dave, who got the origination credit. Stephanie's only regret is that she did not negotiate with Dave to make sure that she received some portion of the credit, which might or might not have been possible given the firm's compensation system).

Stephanie did a great job nurturing her relationship with Dave by approaching him tactfully (and through someone he already knew and trusted), and by sharing with him genuine insights that helped him and his clients. But there is another, very effective way to get other lawyers within your firm to give you access to their clients: Give them access to yours.

When I talked about originating more work from your existing clients, I discussed how you might have some clients that you don't enjoy working with or feel like you could be serving better. Should you dump these clients so that you have more time to find and service the clients for whom you will do your best work? Absolutely not. But you knew that already. A much better approach, and one that fosters greater profitability for you and your firm, is to see if you can partner with other lawyers in your firm for a much more diluted version of a client swap: You give them access to the clients that they view as ideal, and vice versa. I acknowledge that this is a less orthodox approach, and one that requires a finely tuned alignment of interests, but it is an effective tactic that all lawyers should keep in mind.

NEW CLIENTS

The "new client" place is always the last one I go to and here's why: The most favorable estimates show that only about 20% of business comes from new clients. It's no mystery why: Most companies have a roster of existing lawyers that they either love or tolerate, the transactional and/or bureaucratic costs associated with shifting firms is high, and the actual buyer is usually a highly risk-averse lawyer. To say nothing of the fact that when they do find a new firm, they will have to navigate any conflicts that may result.

And yet, most lawyers I know spend the vast majority of their business development time completely focused on bringing in new clients. Now, I'm not advising you to forsake of *ever* bringing in a new client, but I am advising you to devote a proportional amount of the time you spend on business development (i.e., 20% or less) to getting new clients in the door.

The hardest part of getting new clients is finding a way to capture their attention in the first place. Once you do, your clear view of your expertise and how you can solve their problems for them will make getting them in the door seem easy compared to the variety of things you will need to do to make them aware that you even exist. But to share these insights with them, you first have to figure out where they are. And here's how.

FINDING IDEAL CLIENTS OUTSIDE OF YOUR FIRM

There are two ways to find new clients: Proactively cultivating relationships with referral sources, or proactively cultivating relationships directly with potential clients. Whichever approach you decide on; your first step must be to check in with your firm's business development infrastructure. Aligning with your firm's overall strategy is always helpful, but it is truly essential if you want to bring *new* clients to the firm. Your business development professionals will help you realistically assess the market for the type of client you want to bring in, and keep you up to date about any work the firm is doing to expand its reach, some of which may be complementary or even conflict with the new relationships you seek. They can also point you to useful contacts that you can utilize as you cultivate those critical relationships. How exactly do you utilize contacts and cultivate key relationships? I'll cover that later in the book.

CHAPTER 8

PLAN

> "Do what you can with what you have where you are."
> —THEODORE ROOSEVELT

So what is the key to actually originating work? Creating a good plan, and then implementing it systematically and consistently. To do that, you will need to carve out time for business development in your already very busy schedule – and then hold that time sacred. No blowing it off because you have to finish a brief. No blowing it off because someone popped into your office. No blowing it off because you are out of town. If you are serious about business development, you have to do everything you can to literally train your brain to regard the time you spend on business development in the same manner that it regards the time you spend on the partner meeting, the M&A deal blowup, and the client call.

Simply put: If you don't prioritize spending time on business development, you *won't* spend time on business development. I like to think that my strategic insights and sterling wit are why clients love working with me. But in reality, I know a bigger part of the reason is because I not only help them develop their business development plan, I make sure they implement it.

TIME IS NOT A RENEWABLE RESOURCE.

A client once told me a story about a disorganized, inconsiderate litigator he worked with (ever met one of those?), and concluded the story with this frustrated utterance: "It's as though he thinks time is a renewable resource!" How he and his colleague crossed that chasm is a story for another time, but that utterance has stayed with me as a simple and eloquently stated reminder that time is indeed finite. Even for lawyers.

So you see the upside of doing business development, and even have some sense of how you would take your business development efforts to the next level, but how in the name of Justice Ginsburg are you going to squeeze more time in a day? You already cut it as close as you can to maintain some semblance of a personal life, and still feel like you are burning the candle at both ends, borrowing from Peter to pay Paul, and still falling short in most aspects of your life.

Part of this is 100% true. It's just a reflection of the reality of where you are now. By succeeding at business development, you will gain increasing control of your schedule, so you will have more control over your time and how you spend it. *Soon.*

But what if you trained yourself to think of business development not as something to add to your "to do" list, but as the silver bullet it represents: The *one thing* that can give you more job security, income, and control over your professional life. Would you make time for that? I think you would. When you start thinking about your business development work in terms of the benefit it will bring to you instead of "business development" or "blogging" or "networking," it shifts your approach from "just another thing I have to do," to "the one thing I need to do each week to get what I want." It is a powerful way to reframe your thinking, and will help you honor your commitment.

"CREATE" TIME THROUGH THE MAGIC OF DELEGATION.

For most lawyers, once they decide to devote more time to business development, that means they have to figure out how to get the work they were otherwise going to do during that time done. One solution to this is simply effective delegation. Delegation might be the one thing lawyers fear more than business development. There are many complicating factors at play here, but there seem to be two main hurdles to effective delegation in the law firm: Client (or firm) imposed staffing constraints, and weak administrative support.

In an environment where clients are more price-sensitive than ever, billing partners are extremely reluctant to "add too many names to the bill." There are approximately 5,000,000 reasons why that whole approach is a legacy of Biglaw of yore, but that's another book.[21] The bottom line is that you need to free up some of your own time to devote to business development. To do that, you will need to figure out a way to either add more people to the bill, or get the people already on the bill to take over some of your responsibilities.

When I work with lawyers on this issue, they nod and smile, but I know that many of them have zero intention of making any changes to their workload. Some haven't come around to the notion that time is indeed finite, and just figure they'll add more hours to the day (or their day, at least), which is unsustainable. Others don't think they are in a position to affect their workload or the way their cases are staffed.

While that might be true for a very small number of lawyers, I want to call out two underlying assumptions inherent in that second mindset. The first, that you have to maximize the number of hours you bill, because that is the primary way you add value to the firm. While that may be true *for now*, if you really want to take control of your career, you will need to invest some portion of the time that you would otherwise spend on billable work into systematically implementing your business development plan.

The second assumption is that it will take too long to train other lawyers to take over some of your work. The truth is that training will take some time, and you are (most likely) the person who needs to take responsibility for it. But the upsides are significant: The client will be better served by a well-trained and cohesive team, and you will have freed up your time not only for business development, but to do more of the kind of work you want to do.

On the topic of delegation, I am always astounded about how much non-billable time lawyers waste doing administrative tasks that someone else in the firm is *actually paid to do*. I worked with a very senior partner who was terrible at scheduling, but would not let her secretary handle

---

21 Thankfully, one that is already written: Susskind, R.E. (2013). *Tomorrow's Lawyers: An Introduction to Your Future*. Oxford, United Kingdom: Oxford University Press.

her schedule because she "wasn't very good at it." Or the new partner who spent hours creating his own marketing pitches (including presentation decks with 70+ slides, which is just what every busy in-house lawyer loves to see in a pitch) because he thought the marketing people would "take too long and mess it up anyway." And the countless lawyers I know that spend hours doing legal research that ends up as a paragraph or two in an article or speech, when there are literally fleets of associates who could do that work for them in probably half the time.

"CREATE" TIME THROUGH THE MAGIC OF BOUNDARY-SETTING.

Believe it or not, lawyers have a hard time saying "no." At least when it comes to how they function on behalf of themselves (which, as I talked about earlier, is totally different from how they function on behalf of their clients). In particular, this affects their interactions with colleagues and clients. In my experience, the less clarity and confidence a lawyer has about the value they bring to themselves, their firm, and their clients, the more likely they are to struggle with creating and honoring appropriate boundaries. These lawyers are afraid that if they say no or push back, the other person will no longer value them or work with them. Now, law is 100% a customer service business, but if the only service you feel you provide is absolute responsiveness, 24/7 availability, or infinite billable hours, it doesn't sound like a very sustainable or, for that matter, a particularly profitable business to me.

So how much time should you spend on business development? As much as you can, with one caveat: You need to be able to spend the same amount of time each week. So, I encourage clients to start off small, and commit to just one or two hours each week. I also encourage clients to put that time on their calendar and honor it, no matter what.

HOW SHOULD YOU USE YOUR BUSINESS DEVELOPMENT TIME?

At long last, I will talk about tactics like blogging and public speaking and going to cocktail parties! I have buried this part of business development strategy deep in the book because tactics such as these are such a small part of what lawyers really need to do to develop business. Additionally, if you work through this book sequentially, the exact tactics you need to deploy (and how you should be spending your weekly business development time) should be patently obvious. In any case, here we go.

Let's assume that you have committed to spending two hours a week on business development. How should you use that time? In the following three ways.

1. GENERATING INSIGHTS.

Whether you want to get more work from existing clients or new work from new clients, the most important thing you need to be able to do is this: Generate *novel* insights about the particular business challenges facing your ideal clients (that you are uniquely suited to resolve).

To do this, revisit your ideal client composite with a focus on understanding the business challenges they are facing. If you need to get more clarity about those challenges, read their public filings and annual reports, review the reports of analysts that cover their sector, analyze news reports, earnings calls, etc. Think about how larger economic shifts or geopolitical developments might affect companies like them. You could also reach out to people at your firm who already know about the industry or sector, or who might have good firsthand information. Automate the delivery of developments in these areas by setting up news alerts and following key sources on Twitter, LinkedIn, or other relevant social media platforms.

Once you have a better understanding of their business challenges, you need to create novel insights about how *your unique capabilities* can help your ideal clients solve their present and future business challenges.

2. RAISING AWARENESS.

Once you have developed these insights, you need to share them with your ideal clients or the people who can connect you to your ideal clients (this expanded group is also known as your target audience) by using the business development tactics that work best for you. The best way to do that depends on two things: Determining the best way to reach those people, and choosing the approach that works best for you.

The first one is the easiest. The best way to reach those people is to…go to them. So, back you go to your ideal client composite to answer these questions:

- Where do people like your ideal client people congregate?
- Which conferences, associations, industry meetings do they attend? Which clubs do they belong to? Which cultural, sporting, or other non-work event would you find them at? Do they attend CLEs, Bar events, or other professional development sessions?
- Which publications do people like your ideal client read?
- Newspapers? Industry publications? Legal publications?
- Where do people like your ideal client spend time online?
- Which platforms do they use the most (LinkedIn, Twitter, Facebook, etc.)? What blogs do they read? Industry sites?

Once you have answered these questions, you know exactly where to go to reach your target audience. The next question is: Which business development approach works best for you? This question is also easy, and not only because there are only two possible answers, but because most lawyers *already know* the answer. The options here are: Speaking or writing.

If you prefer speaking, whether in one-on-one conversations or to a crowd of 500, you should focus your business development awareness efforts on the opportunities that enable you to speak. That includes the obvious ones: Public speaking opportunities, which your business development team can help you set up. Also consider the less obvious ones: A video blog post, teaching an online seminar, interviews (television, streaming, radio, podcasts, etc.).

If you prefer writing, you should focus your business development awareness efforts on opportunities that enable you to write. I am sure you are familiar with the obvious writing outlets, but I encourage you to differentiate yourself by being creative: Write an e-book, get quoted by a newspaper, comment on other blogs, send out short, practical notes to clients about how current events may affect their business.

Whether you choose to focus on writing or speaking, just make sure that you select your platforms based only on the access they will give you to your target audience. As to content, keep it exclusively focused on the insights that your target audience will value. This will differentiate you as someone who always has something relevant to say, instead of someone who just takes up their very valuable time.

3. ENGAGING STRATEGICALLY.

Once your target audience knows who you are and that you have the exact solutions to the business challenges they are facing, the next step is to develop a relationship with them. The key to developing relationships with prospective clients is to focus on building an authentic connection, keeping in touch, and being sure to deliver valuable insights in every interaction.

If you worked through the rest of this book, the authentic connection piece is a no-brainer. Your ideal client is someone who does work that you find compelling and likely has interests that overlap with yours. The trickier part is maintaining that authenticity through consistent follow up that both keeps you top of their mind *and* continually delivers novel insights to them. The easiest way to do this is to use a CRM (client/customer relationship management) system, which tracks your interactions with contacts and reminds you to follow up at prescribed intervals. This will help you follow up consistently, so that when your prospective client needs your help, you won't be reaching out to them out of the blue. To ensure you are always delivering novel and valuable insights during these follow ups, you should automate the process by which you stay current on the business challenges your ideal clients are facing, as discussed previously.

It goes without saying that meeting in person is the most effective way to truly connect with another person. So, another aspect of engaging strategically is to find opportunities for you and your prospective clients (or your colleagues who can connect you to them) to get together. If you live in the same area as your prospective client, consider inviting them to something compelling, namely, anything other than lunch or yet another client training seminar hosted by your firm. If you want to meet with a client who is located elsewhere, well, plan a trip to make it happen. And if you are going to visit with one prospective client in another city, why not visit with two or more on the same trip?

HOW WILL YOU MAKE SURE YOU DO ANYTHING?

Another key part of your business development plan will be to build in a system of accountability. You know yourself best, so you will know which one will be most effective. Here is an overview of some of the systems I have seen lawyers implement successfully:

SELF-ACCOUNTABILITY

At the end of each week, evaluate your business development efforts. Identify what you did, what you said you would do but didn't get to, what went well and what didn't. Establish new priorities and update your plan for the following week. Repeat weekly.

TECHNOLOGICAL ACCOUNTABILITY

Use a CRM, project management, or other type of software or app that helps you track what you're doing, and more importantly, reminds you about what you should be doing.

COMMUNITY ACCOUNTABILITY

Create a group of like-minded lawyers (or see if your firm knows of such a group) and come together weekly for mutual support. A great example of this is a group of women lawyers in Los Angeles, who joined together to encourage each other to develop business.[22] As the women became more and more successful, they essentially created their own internal

---

22 Sullivan, C. (2016). These Nine Women Lawyers Love Two Things: Dancing, and Makin' it Rain. Retrieved September 13, 2016, from https://bol.bna.com/these-nine-women-lawyers-love-two-things-dancing-and-makin-it-rain.

referral network, which led them to even higher levels of success and professional satisfaction.

PARTNER ACCOUNTABILITY

Depending on your relationship with your business development or marketing professionals, this would be a great and natural role for them to play. It is exactly like group accountability, but in a one to one setting. Shameless self-promotion: Law firms hire me to provide lawyers with *precisely* this kind of accountability.

CHAPTER 9

SELL

> "If I had asked people what they wanted,
> they would have said 'faster horses.'"
> – HENRY FORD

First, the bad news: It's time to take everything you've learned so far, and actually develop business, by which I mean sell legal services. Seeing as you have stuck with me for this long, I feel compelled to let you in on a little secret. This step – the selling – is by far the most important step, and skipping it is the number one reason lawyers don't originate work. Did you catch that? *Most lawyers don't originate work because they don't sell their services to prospective clients.*

Now, the good news: The most effective way to *sell* legal services is identical to the most effective way to *deliver* legal services. Did you catch that one too? All you have to do is interact with your potential clients in the same way you interact with your existing clients, and your chances of bringing in the work go up dramatically. I guess I probably should have told you that in the beginning (but let's be honest, you and I both know that you would have stopped reading right then and there).

Here's how to translate your client *service* skills into client *acquisition* skills.

SELL LIKE YOU WILL DELIVER.[23]

RESEARCH

What's the very first thing you do when you work on a new matter? Research.

I already talked about the research piece in my discussion about how to generate useful insights (Chapter 8). So, by the time you get to the sales conversation, the bulk of your research will be completed. You will know the client's unique business challenges, how they are impacted by external events, and even (hopefully) the internal dynamics that affect the client personally. The only other topic you need to research is the exact scope of the business challenges the client is facing and *the legal tools they will need solve those challenges.* You'll notice that this is the first time I am recommending you even think about a legal solution to a client's business problem.

ASK OPEN-ENDED QUESTIONS.

What's the second thing you do when you work on a new matter? Ask open-ended questions.

You've done your research and have a good view into the client's business challenges, and probably have an idea about which legal tools they need/want to solve those challenges. At this juncture, it is absolutely critical that you put aside your instinct to demonstrate your technical competency of the law, eloquence, or Mensa-caliber intellect.

Instead, you need to completely focus on asking the client open-ended questions with the goal of – get this – helping *the client* think through the contours of their challenge. This is not the time to demonstrate your mastery of the arcane by asking 800 questions about issues that are more than likely of no import to the client. This is not the time to secure "the alpha role" by taking charge of the conversation. This is the time to demonstrate to the client that you are a different breed of lawyer – a lawyer who is completely focused on them *and their problem*, a lawyer whose goal

---

23 Maister, D. H., Green, C. H., & Galford, R. M. (2000). *The trusted advisor.* New York: Free Press.

is to *partner with them* to help them think through their issues, prioritize what's important, and find a practical, cost-effective solution, a lawyer who, quite simply, they will enjoy working with over the long-term.

LISTEN DEEPLY.

Lawyers are simply the worst listeners. As a former lawyer, I speak from a place of firsthand knowledge of my own inherent challenges. Even now, as a coach, I aim to spend about 80% of my time listening. My average is closer to 60%, and to get there, I often have to physically force myself to just keep my mouth closed.

Deep listening plays a critical role in client engagement. Subconsciously, the speaker feels more connected to the listener, which is great. But even more powerfully, the less you talk, the more the client will – and that is how you will learn a lot more about the nature of their problem, what they have done to try to solve it themselves, and what they really need going forward. This kind of interaction is not only useful for engaging clients, it is a great way to make sure that you and the client remain on the same page throughout the engagement, which turns out to be the best way to get additional engagements.

FOCUS ON THE CLIENT'S BUSINESS PROBLEM, NOT YOUR LEGAL SOLUTIONS.

I might be beating a dead horse here, but I just cannot emphasize this point enough. Every single time you interact with clients or prospective clients, you have to stay completely focused on the business problem they are facing. They really, truly already know what a great lawyer you are. They also already know the major legal issues that they need to think about. What they *don't know* is how to solve their current and future business problems in the most efficient, cost-effective way possible.

Here's a comparison of two scenarios that illustrate contrasting approaches to a sales opportunity with a prospective client. Bill, a young partner who works on employment discrimination cases, identified Helen as an ideal client – and stayed in touch with her after a mutual contact introduced them. Bill invited Helen to a baseball game, both because of their shared love of baseball, and because he had heard some rumblings about possible personnel changes at her company. When the time seemed opportune, Bill raised the issue with Helen.

SCENARIO 1

Helen: It is such a challenge to know how to handle performance management issues with our folks who are approaching retirement age. We really value their knowledge and contributions, but for the ones who underperform, we're finding it really hard to help them, and it feels like we have run out of options. My client would like to fire some of them, but we're concerned about the risk associated with that approach.

Bill: That is a really complicated problem. I was just reading a really interesting article in *HR Today* about how the EEOC is really stepping up its enforcement and investigation activities. A very scary time to think about firing anyone who is over 55. A lot of my clients are facing these issues, and I have helped a lot of them navigate through this exact scenario. In fact, I gave a presentation at a national conference on this topic and wrote a companion article. I would be happy to share those with you.

Helen: Okay– that would be helpful. Thank you.
[Back to watching the game]

SCENARIO 2

Helen: It is such a challenge to know how to handle performance management issues with our folks who are approaching retirement age. We really value their knowledge and contributions, but for the ones who underperform, we're finding it really hard to help them, and it feels like we have run out of options. My client would like to fire some of them, but we're concerned about the risk associated with that approach.

Bill: Yes, the risk there is definitely something to think about. What's the name of your client?

Helen: Bob.

Bill: How many people would Bob like to let go?

Helen: At most, five.

Bill: Why is he focused on those five?

Helen: Well, this is confidential, right?

Bill: Absolutely.

Helen: Three of them are truly disruptive, and have not contributed to the overall goals of the group in a long time. We have them each on a performance plan, which they are pretty much phoning in. So, for those three, I actually feel pretty comfortable with what Bob wants to do.

Bill: What about the other two?

Helen: (Sigh). That is kind of where the rubber meets the road. The other two have each had some – in my view – extenuating family circumstances that I don't think Bob has thought through sufficiently.

Bill: What do you mean?

Helen: I am afraid that Bob is being rash, and throwing those two over the side with the other three because he really wants to clear out all the "dead weight" at once, and get his numbers up fast.

Bill: Do you have any sense of what boost letting these five people go will give to Bob's numbers?

Helen: No, but it would be interesting to know...

Bill: If there was litigation, would the fees, fines or settlement amounts come out of your budget, or out of Bob's budget?

Helen: Mine.

Bill: Have you guys had any other issues in this space in the last few years?

Helen: No, this is new for us as a company. At least since I've been there.

Bill: How long have you been there?

Helen: About five years.

Bill: Does Bob pre-date you?

Helen: Oh yes. He's been there forever.

Bill: Do you and Bob work well together?

Helen: Yes and no. I like him personally, but I think he sometimes views me as someone who creates unnecessary obstacles. Which is really unfair, as I am the HR lawyer for Pete's sake, and I have saved the company tons of money by preventing situations like this from blowing up.

———

This conversation could go on for a long time, but I can end it here because the contrast in approaches (and results) is already clear. Let's figure out what made the difference between the two.

ISSUE IDENTIFICATION VS. PLUMBING THE DEPTHS OF THE PROBLEM

In the first scenario, Bill does what lawyers do best (and naturally). He has used his well-honed analytical skills to identify all the red flags that are calling out to him in Helen's very brief overview of her problem. This is an essential skill set for the practice of law, but really works *against* lawyers in business development. Helen already knows she has a problem, and, being a lawyer herself, has probably already spotted the issues that Bill called out. Granted, Helen's knowledge is not as specialized as Bill's, so her depth on the issue is more limited, but in the first scenario, Bill has not necessarily told Helen anything she didn't already know. More critically, Bill also missed an opportunity to genuinely connect with Helen, so that she could start to view him as a trusted partner to help her sort out this problem.

SUPERFICIAL PROBLEM SOLVING VS. AUTHENTIC LEGAL COUNSELING

In the first scenario, Bill implies that all Helen needs to do to solve her problem is to hire Bill to tell her whether she should fire a nebulous group of underperforming old people. Helen raised the topic with Bill, not to see if Bill would be interested in solving her problem for her (that is Bill's goal, not Helen's), but to actually try to work through a problem she's having that she may or may not be able to solve herself.

In the second scenario, Bill puts his goals and initial conclusions aside, and forces himself to listen deeply to Helen. This allows the two of them to uncover everything he will need to convince her that if this proves to be a problem she can't solve for herself, the only person she would want to hire to solve that problem is Bill. How does he do that?

- He asks open-ended questions and exhibits genuine curiosity about Helen's answers.
- He looks for a personal connection.
- He leaves out breadcrumbs – little nuggets that help Helen think about her problem in another way, which may or may not help her solve her problem herself.
- He stays focused on Helen's problem, instead of his solution.

This approach is inherently unique because it is based completely on Bill and Helen's interaction. This help builds the case in Helen's mind that if she does need to hire a lawyer, Bill would be her first (and maybe) only choice. This type of differentiation is critical in today's market for lawyers who do not want to compete on price. And the only way to avoid doing that (and the fee deflation, discount demands, and alternative pricing discussions that come with it), is to demonstrate the unique value you can bring to your prospective client.

CHAPTER 10

ANALYZE

"We are what we repeatedly do. Excellence,
then, is not an act, but a habit."
—ARISTOTLE

Second only to action, analyzing the effectiveness of your business development efforts is a key intervention for most lawyers. How do you measure such a thing? In three steps.

First, what did you do and how long did it take? Record.

Second, what was the result? Reflect.

Third, what should you change (if anything)? Rework.

RECORD

To lawyers already accustomed to accounting for their time in six-minute increments, recording what they did and how long it took is fairly intuitive. But much like recording your time, if you don't commit to doing it, it won't happen. So I encourage everyone to create some type of system that helps them track their efforts in the simplest, lowest-tech way possible.

REFLECT

The second step is the most crucial, and the one most lawyers are most likely to skip. After you have recorded your efforts, reflect on them and see what you think. What's working? What isn't? What do you enjoy doing? What took longer than you expected? Was it a good use of your time?

Take Minerva, for example. Minerva loved public speaking and was truly great at it. She had a good topic and her business development coordinator had no trouble lining up plenty of relevant speaking opportunities. But when we talked about her overall business development strategy, Minerva was frustrated because she felt like she was doing everything she could to develop business – including all of things I laid out in this book – but she was getting nowhere. I asked her to record all the time she spent on her public speaking, including the preparation, the travel, the downtime, etc.

All told, she discovered that she was spending an average of 10 hours each month on this approach, or about 2.5 hours each week. That seemed like a reasonable amount of time for her to spend to achieve her business development goals, so no problem there.

Then I asked her to list the results that she achieved that she could definitively link to the public speaking work. She had a number of great results: Relationships at four different companies that she was cultivating, and an invitation to do one pitch, which she really enjoyed, although she did not ultimately get the work. Then I asked her to total up all of the time it took her to get those results, and the tally astonished her: The return on her investment of approximately 220 hours of effort (10 hours a month for almost 2 years), was four new relationships and one pitch.

She decided this was not a cost-benefit analysis that was coming out in her favor, which her enabled to (very) quickly move from a place of frustration (I am terrible at this!) to one of action (What should I do differently to get better results?).

REWORK

Once Minerva realized that she spent the equivalent of one month of billable time on a tactic that yielded few results (and no bookable revenue), she knew something needed to change, but she wasn't sure what. Minerva's instinct was to throw the proverbial baby out with the bath water and adjust all components of her business development simultaneously. Her instinct was to give up on public speaking, find a new target audience, and market a different aspect of her experience. Her instinct was wrong.

For this third step, lawyers have to tap into something they have in spades (strategic analytical thinking) and something they don't (patience).

Once you realize your efforts have not produced the results you expected them to, the next step is *not* to take a totally different tack. Rather, you need to suspend your sense of urgency, and the reflex to make up for lost time, and focus on teasing out which aspects of your business development strategy you want to keep and build on, and which ones you are going to let go.

I encourage lawyers to approach this step as a question: How do I change my business development tactics to make them more effective? This helps you automatically engage your strategic thinking skills, and things often fall into place pretty quickly. There is one caveat: The analysis needs to start with identifying both what you are good at, and what you enjoy doing.

In Minerva's case, her preference for public speaking signaled a real strength in connecting with other people, and generating the energy that goes along with that. So varying her tactic (public speaking) did not seem to be the place to start. Similarly, the way she showcased her own expertise, along with the way she was leveraging her firm's platform, also seemed to be working in her favor. She was pulling many business development levers really effectively: She knew what she was selling (expertise) and she liked the business development tactic she was using (public speaking), and her firm was very supportive of her efforts. Once we took those things off the table, Minerva realized her message wasn't resonating with her prospective clients. She had gotten so wrapped up in the fun of public speaking that she lost sight of the need to shape her presentations to address her client's business challenges (rather than her legal solutions). Minerva committed to adjusting her message, and seeing how tweaking the way she pulled that single lever of business development would impact her outcomes. I told Minerva she had 90 days to make that assessment.

THE MAGIC OF 90 DAYS.

Is a 90-day trial period arbitrary? Yes. And so is billing in 6 minute incre-ments (which clients adore, by the way). The real magic behind the trial period is not its length, although even in an industry that moves at such a glacial pace as does the law, 90 days is truly enough time to collect data that will help you understand whether something is working. The magic is in creating a hard deadline for you to evaluate whether or not something is working for you. It not only makes sense on paper, but it actually creates a shift in the way you approach business development. Instead of casting about uncertainly, pulling all the levers up and down like an organ player at a particularly frenzied concert, you can create a deliberate approach to business development out of the chaos. If you were going to talk to yourself about it (and really, where would you find better company?), it might sound something like this:

> For the next 90 days, this is my plan. At the end of the 90 days, I am going to look back to see what results I have achieved. If those results are not what I would like them to be, I am going to evaluate which aspect of my plan seems to be the weakest. I will change that one thing and create a modified plan, which I will execute for 90 days.

And so on.

I know no one will be surprised by this, but this approach necessarily in-cludes the concept of failure. Yes, failure. There, I said it. I know I have thrown out a lot of reasons why I think lawyers struggle with business de-velopment, but this is 100%, truly, without a doubt, the biggest hurdle.[24]

Ever since they got their first A, lawyers have built their entire lives around getting to the next one, or put more bluntly – avoiding failure. When I talk about the honor of failure with lawyers, they laugh nervously

---

24 Acknowledging that failure is a part of learning is a key aspect of a growth mindset, which correlates highly with personal and professional success. Dweck, C. S. (2006). *Mindset: The new psychology of success.* New York: Random House.

and acknowledge (philosophically) that why, yes, of course that makes sense. Then they often go on to tell me that they are well-inured to failure. In fact, they spend their entire working existence duking it out with opposing lawyers who are doing everything in their power to defeat them, because as we all know, law is not a win-win proposition.

Constant immersion in this adversarial environment has a profound impact on lawyers. But there is a distinction between the bruising that lawyers endure day in and day out on behalf of their clients, which is mandatory, and the bruising they get from the trial and error that necessarily goes along with business development, which feels "optional." While lawyers feel terrible when the other side wins a motion, or gets a concession they didn't want to give, they can at least transfer some of the responsibility to the client, the judge, the other side, or the e-discovery vendor for that failure.

In contrast, when you're going out in the world offering to help clients solve their problems and you spend lots of time and energy in trying to do just that – and then nothing comes of it? Now that's something that feels a lot more like the f-word. Just the thought of that – of putting yourself out there and getting rejected, even though you are smart, went to a good law school, work at a prestigious law firm, do great work, and are really interested in helping the client – and really, really need this case to come through so that you can stop being afraid of getting fired, spend more time with your kids, and get the bonuses you need to pay off your law school loans and save for retirement. Now those are some high stakes. And even the very thought of failure, under those circumstances, is devastating.

So, how do you get past this tremendous hurdle? You acknowledge you are going to fail. You steel yourself ahead of time that your first few meetings, presentations, blog posts, etc. are going to really and truly suck. You will say the wrong thing, split an infinitive, speak to a room of 500 with food in your teeth. You will. And that is fine. And you know what? You already know that. It's probably what is holding you back.

So let's just build failure into the plan. Crazy, right? For lawyers, assuming you are going to blow up early and often gives you the permission you need to try something new. Here's the amazing upside (and the main reason I love working with lawyers) – lawyers are the fastest learners in the world. While nearly everything I have talked about in this book is alien to most lawyers, once they wrap their brains around the concepts *and* decide these concepts will help them do what they want do to, they get up and running so fast that I have to do everything I can to keep up with them. So take heart, all the bumps and bruises, worries, fears, and insecurities that are going to be screaming in your ear and hitting you over the head are merely a signal that you are pushing yourself to the edge of what you know.

Perhaps Rocky Balboa said it best:

It ain't about how hard you hit: it's about how hard you can get hit, and keep moving forward. It's how much you can take, and keep moving forward. That's how winning is done.

CONCLUSION

STEP INTO THE ARENA (I'LL COME WITH YOU)

It is not the critic who counts; not the man who
points out how the strong man stumbles, or where
the doer of deeds could have done them better.
The credit belongs to the man who is actually in
the arena, whose face is marred by dust and sweat
and blood; who strives valiantly; who errs, who
comes short again and again, because there is no
effort without error and shortcoming; but who does
actually strive to do the deeds; who knows great
enthusiasms, the great devotions; who spends himself
in a worthy cause; who at the best knows in the end
the triumph of high achievement, and who at the
worst, if he fails, at least fails while daring greatly,
so that his place shall never be with those cold and
timid souls who neither know victory nor defeat.

— THEODORE ROOSEVELT, PARIS,
FRANCE (APRIL 23, 1910).

The above is an excerpt from Teddy Roosevelt's famous *Citizen in a Republic* speech, which he delivered about a year after he left office.[25] I chose to end the book with it for two reasons.

25 Roosevelt, T. (1910). The Man in the Arena. Retrieved September 13, 2016, from
http://www.theodorerooseveltcenter.org/Learn-About-TR/TR-Encyclopedia/Culture-and-

First, his exhortations about the sacredness of the liberties and profound responsibilities we all share as citizens in a republic reminds me of the noble and just purpose at the heart of our profession. That purpose is why I and so many other lawyers I know went to law school, and it's inspiring to get back in touch with that purpose every so often.

But his deeper point – that to achieve something you truly desire, you have to strive for it, step into the arena for it, every single day – is exactly what I help lawyers do. Getting "marred by dust and sweat and blood" (or the 21st century equivalent) is not easy. But the only way to get what you actually want – instead of what you can have, or what someone else will give you – is to go *through* the hard part to the other side. That's where I come in. I have stepped into the arena with lots of attorneys and provided them with the insight, motivation, and support they needed to get to the other side. It *will not* be easy, but it *will* be worth it.

Society/Man-in-the-Arena.aspx.

YOUR TURN

I always enjoy hearing from lawyers, and would particularly value your thoughts and insights about business development and your own experiences at Biglaw. My goal is to bring the best and most up to date practices to my clients, and learning from other lawyers is one of the best ways to do that. You can reach me at mcr@mcrstratgies.com, (202) 394-5091 or through my website: mcrstrategies.com.

See you in the arena,

Michelle

ACKNOWLEDGEMENTS

The list of people that helped me write this book has to start with my favorite lawyer, Edward Richards. His profound insights and embodiment of all that is right with the legal profession (to say nothing of his constant verbal *tête-à-tête*, and unwavering support in all of my myriad endeavors) makes me hope that our boys not only inherited his looks, but his very essence.

I am also eternally grateful to my two favorite non-lawyers, Harry and John, who constantly remind me of the wonders and joy of the simplest things in life.

I am also extraordinarily grateful to my long-suffering parents, Margaret and Malcolm Cotter, for basically everything, but in this context, for modeling a genuine love of a job well done and the benefits of finding your highest and best use – no matter what.

To my amazing group of friends: Your integrity, kindness, and boundless love makes even the bumpiest parts of the road of life manageable. I am truly excited to grow old(er) with you. A special shout out to MY ideal client, my sistah from another mistah, Clement, J.

To Dick Beckler, who taught me everything about true leadership, loyalty, and how to thrive in Biglaw.

To Ed Han, who painstakingly showed me the power of always delivering more than you promise and the sheer joy that comes from mastery of the law.

To Kathy Sparrough, who knew this was the path for me before I did (and uncharacteristically kept that opinion to herself).

Finally, to all the lawyers I have the privilege to know – your work paves the way forward, leaving a more noble profession in its wake. Keep on rockin'.

ABOUT THE AUTHOR

M ichelle Cotter Richards, a former Biglaw litigator and in-house counsel, draws on her years of experience coaching Biglaw attorneys to teach them a new, more effective approach to Biglaw business development. Michelle empowers lawyers to create an efficient, sustainable approach to business development based on where their unique capabilities intersect with the needs of their clients. Michelle teaches lawyers how to regain control of their time and their professional trajectory and consistently execute a business development strategy that works for them.

Although Michelle spent most of her career with Howrey LLP, she also worked as an Assistant General Counsel for MCI, Inc., and as the number two lawyer for a privately held media company. She received her J.D. with Honors from The George Washington University Law School, and her B.A. in American Studies from Fordham University.

Michelle is passionate about helping Biglaw firms and attorneys utilize emotional intelligence to create more profitable, sustainable, and satisfying practices. She is a co-creator of the D.C. Bar's groundbreaking emotional intelligence training program for lawyers and speaks frequently about Biglaw leadership development and business development issues to organizations such as the National Association for Law Placement (NALP), the Association of Legal Administrators (ALA), and various law firms, law schools, and legal departments.

Michelle is an ICF-certified coach, and is certified to administer the EQ-i 2.0 emotional intelligence assessment, the Myers-Briggs Type Indicator (MBTI), and the DISC individual and team behavioral instrument.

She lives in Washington, DC, with her husband and two boys.

NOTES

NOTES

NOTES

NOTES

NOTES

NOTES

www.ingramcontent.com/pod-product-compliance
Lightning Source LLC
Chambersburg PA
CBHW021411170526
45164CB00002B/594